A FIELD GUIDE FO___

When Jim Peacock speaks...listen! He's got the pulse of career changers, tapped into thought leaders nationwide, listens to clients and career practitioners deeply, and translates and makes meaning like few others. Jim's ability to articulate what's not said or written about career development pushes my practice ahead. With years of direct practice experience Jim's insights clears the air, filters the noise, and offers wise structure to career coaching.

—Rich Feller Ph.D, former NCDA president (2012–13),
professor, entrepreneur, and consultant

Jim Peacock is one of the first people I recommend when someone I know is in need of career help. He strikes a nice balance of support and challenge, inspiration and practicality. As a leader in our field, he shares his strengths and skills with peers to raise the level of practice across the profession. I have had the privilege of seeing him work in various settings across various platforms and am amazed by how his humor, genuine caring, and passion for helping other thrive shines through.

Every time we have interacted or I've read his work, I always come away with a new way of thinking about things or new things to try with clients. I cannot recommend Jim more highly!

—Lisa Severy, director of career services, University of Colorado
Boulder and former NCDA president (2013–2014)

Jim Peacock brings passion and knowledge to the field of career development. As a highly skilled practitioner and trainer, he truly understands clients and their needs. As a seasoned presenter and trainer, Jim consistently develops materials meaningful to practitioners. His work is always on topic, high quality, and timely!

Jim's work in numerous settings with a diverse client base and leadership roles in career development associations also speaks to his reputation and service. He has also received recognition for his work from the National Career Development Association and National Academic Advising Association.

It is my pleasure to recommend A Field Guide for Career Practitioners *to you!*

—Dr. Constance J. Pritchard, president, The Pritchard Group,
NCDA fellow, master trainer, and instructor

To advise private clients, students and post grads, and job seekers who attend public career centers, you need to be well versed in job-search tactics. Jim Peacock falls under this category. I've known Jim for more than six years, having connected with him on LinkedIn, and I can say with certainty that Jim has the credentials and expertise to teach career practitioners at any level.

Whether it is his online career training or individual counseling, Jim is at the top of the career development industry. I had the pleasure of taking one of Jim's online seminars and found it thought-provoking and valuable. I've also benefited from his tutelage in leading a LinkedIn class he offers his clients. A Field Guide for Career Practitioners: Helping Clients Create Their Next Move *is a must read for anyone who is in the career business at any level.*

—Bob McIntosh, career strategist, MassHire Lowell Career Center

Jim Peacock is one of the most highly respected career services professionals in the United States. Jim is a nationally known career development expert, a prolific career blog writer, and an excellent instructor nationally certified by the National Career Development Association.

Jim is a true thought leader; his career advice is rooted in common sense and reality, not vague generalities based on the prevailing conventional wisdom. There are so many "career experts" dispensing advice, but having worked closely with Jim and having taken his course which led me to my Global Career Development Facilitator (GCDF) credential, I know for sure he is a leader and an expert in the career advising field.

—Rich Grant, GCDF, remote career advisor for an online university,
former president of the Maine College Career Consortium

It was no accident that I discovered Jim Peacock. In looking for quality, affordable professional development for myself and for the Wisconsin Career Development Association I had the luck to be introduced to Jim's work. I've had the opportunity to learn from Jim both in person and online. His presentations and classes always contain thoughtful, relevant content.

Jim does a fabulous job facilitating connections between participants whether face-to-face or at a distance. I use exercises and concepts learned from Jim with clients seeking career change. I've known Jim for over eight years and will continue

to seek out his workshops for my own professional growth and recommend him to others in the career development field.

—Moira G. Kelley, senior counselor/communications coordinator, UW-Madison Division of Continuing Studies

I have known Jim Peacock for over a decade and have worked with him in professional associations, taken his online seminars, and participated in his workshops. I truly believe he is one of the best career development professionals in the country. Jim is a consummate colleague and extremely passionate about helping further the skills and knowledge of his fellow colleagues through his workshops and online seminars. He is one of my go to resources when I have questions that I need to answer or learn techniques to help my clients more effectively.

—James Westhoff, M.Ed., CCC (Certified Career Counselor), director, Career Services, Husson University

Jim introduced and trained me in the Motivated Skills Card Sort, and I continue to use this assessment in my work with students. He provides thorough and enthusiast training, and I was immediately sold on this assessment after completing the training. I use it regularly in my work as a career counselor and coach and have found it to be a very valuable tool in working with students.

Jim is delightful to work with, and clearly is working his magic as a career professional.

—Renée Beaupré White, job and career coach

At some point theory for career development needs to be put to practice. No one is a better suited guide than Jim to show clear, easy, and accessible ways for one to jump from "career philosopher" to "career practitioner" and begin helping clients immediately. I met Jim a few years in my career and I am glad that I did. As a co-worker and CDF instructor, Jim taught me how to become self-sufficient in developing new techniques and strategies for working with the wide variety of students I see.

Because of my experiences working with Jim, I feel prepared- and eager- to tackle new challenges with clients because I have a trail map of strategies that anyone can navigate. WARNING: Jim's enthusiasm for this kind of

work is contagious. If you catch the bug, you may display the symptoms of an expert practitioner for the rest of your life.

—Jordan Bell, Career Services at Columbus College of Art & Design

Jim Peacock has become iconic for offering practical strategies to deliver career development services. He challenges assumptions and promotes theoretical models and approaches his work with compassion and wisdom. As an NCDA colleague, I have observed Jim's capacity to captivate an audience with his engaging teaching and insightful techniques.

—Dr. Sharon Givens, director of Visions Counseling and Career Center LLC, NCDA board of directors, trustee for private practice, business/industry & agencies

Jim Peacock's career spans academic advising, community colleges, universities, and leadership roles in career development professional associations, so he's well-qualified to tackle the wide range of topics in this book.

With gentle encouragement to reflect on and challenge our current ways of working, Jim explains how, from his own experience, our biases (yes, we all have them) can get in the way of effective counseling. He also discusses the importance of intentionally talking less, in order to help our clients find their own answers within themselves.

Elsewhere, Jim reinforces the importance of networking and self-care, with tips on how to help clients (and ourselves) get better at these essential skills. In particular, Jim identifies the benefits of embracing and teaching mindfulness practices, advice that I believe will resonate with many coaches and other career practitioners.

If you've been considering going into private practice, you will naturally want to read what Jim has to say, from the heart, on this topic. Other readers, like myself, will be engaged by Jim's thoughtful advice on the topic of professional development, and I'm eager to listen to the TED talks and podcasts that he recommends.

The focus of this book is on practical guidance for fellow career professionals, brought to life with illustrations from Jim's own work, which will inform and inspire readers who are new to the career development profession and also pro-

vide even seasoned coaches and counselors with some new suggestions for taking our practice to the next level.

—Sabrina Woods, holistic career/life coach
& consultant, www.sabrina-woods.com

Yes, at some point in the very near future, someone will look your clients up online and most likely they will find your LinkedIn profile. Take the time and effort to follow Jim Peacock's recommendations, step by step. Your clients only have one chance to make a great first impression and this will help you get them there!

In fact, the entire book will help you help your clients. Jim has a wonderful way of mixing important statistics and stories to emphasize his points.

—Hannah Morgan, job search and social media strategist, careersherpa.net

This book represents an exciting new addition to the literature addressing career interventions. It incorporates the most current thinking regarding career development and presents this information in a very accessible and useful way. The use of concepts honoring positive uncertainty, serendipity, career chaos, and hope-action theory offers a foundation from which the most relevant career interventions emerge. This is a real strength for those seeking to provide innovative career strategies.

Another strength of A Field Guide for Career Practitioners: Helping Clients Create Their Next Move *resides in Peacock's thorough coverage of social media as a vehicle for career intervention. It is critical that career practitioners make full use of social media but that they do so in thoughtful, intentional, and effective ways. This book offers strategies that guide practitioners in accomplishing this goal.*

Finally, I'm struck by the way in which the author's passion for his work and for communicating this to fellow practitioners resounds throughout the book. The combination of all of the above results in a resource that readers will find both helpful and enjoyable to read.

—Spencer Niles, president, NCDA (2003–2004; 2018–2019),
dean and professor, College of William & Mary

A FIELD GUIDE

for

CAREER PRACTITIONERS

HELPING CLIENTS CREATE THEIR NEXT MOVE

Jim Peacock

Thank You

I am who I am because of all the people I have come into contact with, and I want to thank a few of them here.

First, my dad. He has been a huge influence on my philosophy of "honoring all jobs" in my work. He was president of a small-to-mid-size bank in downriver Detroit where I grew up. He could have moved out to one of the local islands where "all the rich people went." He could have hung out only with other professionals like him. What I saw were many of his friends who were carpenters, plumbers, electricians, masons, store owners, and more. He taught me that all jobs are valuable and should be respected.

I am grateful to my wife Deborah for supporting me on this Peak-Careers Consulting adventure. Even though she was nervous about me leaving a full-time position with benefits and a regular paycheck, she supported me. And I promised her that no matter what, we would still do "date night" each week. And we have...although we did have a few months that were pretty tight for money. Thank you honey.

My brother Mark is also my best friend and has been one of my biggest supporters. He is also the person who encouraged me to leave my position in order to take the leap into my own business. Most importantly, he introduced me to the idea of starting each day in thoughtful meditation and occasionally taking a day-long retreat to leave behind technology and the busyness of life. His support and never-ending love is why mindfulness is so important in my life and work.

Rees Hughes has been a true friend, mentor, and confidant for nearly four decades. We met at Seattle University when he was the Director of Student Activities. I was working in the Registrar's Office but wanted to get into student activities, so I asked if I could volunteer and help him out. We grew a friendship that includes about 1,700 miles of the Pacific Crest Trail together—mostly in 120-400 mile sections. We keep our friendship going through regular Zoom sessions that keep us connected (he lives in California and I live in Maine). He has talked me through some of my most difficult professional times, advised me on numerous issues, and modeled for me thoughtful, intelligent responses to situations. My ENFP response is often a quick response with lots of talking and he has helped me be more thoughtful.

To my entire Peak-Careers Advisory Board who over the years has provided support, suggestions, nudges, guidance, and more throughout this great adventure—thank you Kim Gustafson, Rob Seeman, Dale Stair, Rich Grant, Mary Sweeney, Sabrina Woods, Jordan Bell, Rees Hughes, and Karen Chopra.

And finally, thanks to the following people who reviewed drafts of this book and gave me insight and perspective to make it much better each time I edited: Mark Danaher, Hannah Morgan, Rees Hughes, and Bill Stone.

There are many more people who have supported and encouraged me throughout my life and career. I can't possibly list them all here. You know who you are and I am forever grateful.

Table of Contents

Why I Do What I Do

D uring his tenure as chief of the U.S. Forest Service, Gifford Pinchot helped triple the nation's forest reserves and shaped the agency's guiding principle to "provide the greatest good for the greatest amount of people in the long run." (Read more at http://bit.ly/peakcareers97).

I am a forestry major. I've never worked in forestry—never will. But Gifford Pinchot's statement above has stuck with me throughout my entire life. As a school counselor I loved the career conversations I had with students but realized that my "reach" doing career counseling was limited to one-on-one. If I really wanted to "provide the greatest good for the greatest amount of people in the long run," it would come from helping other career service providers improve their skills.

In 1999 I heard about the Facilitating Career Development (FCD) class developed by the National Occupational Information Coordinating Committee (NOICC) and in partnership with National Career Development Association. This 120-hour course recognized that many people were delivering career services with little or no training. I jumped at the opportunity to be trained to teach this class.

I have been teaching the FCD class annually since 2001, and that was the beginning of Peak-Careers Consulting. This was my chance to reach more career practitioners and really help them to help others. Hundreds of people have taken the FCD class from me, but I know that I have affected the lives of thousands, maybe tens of thousands, of people by helping many career practitioners improve their services. Just writing that statement motivates me.

Watching those "ah ha" moments in my class, workshops, or online seminars feels magical. There is always more to learn, and I believe we learn best by taking action and then discussing the results of that action with

1

other like-minded career practitioners. **I hope this book inspires you to take action, continue your professional development, and discuss what you've learned—with the end result of being a better career practitioner.**

The first seven chapters of this book detail how I approach working with my clients, with some insight to my philosophy of career development. I believe that often our main purpose when working with our clients or students is to help them make a mindset change (**Chapter 1**). Too many people have trouble getting out of their "vortex of negativity," i.e., only seeing the negative in their career and life. We can help people see the big picture, take the long view, and look at their current situation from a different perspective.

Chapter 2 introduces my philosophy of "intentional serendipity," which has been greatly influenced by the work of Krumboltz, Levin, and Mitchell's Happenstance Learning Theory. Intentional serendipity is taking action and being open to discovering something by accident. It happens all the time—more often if you look for it.

When working with my clients the first thing I want to hear from them is their "value-added statement"—the five or six essentials things they want everyone to know about themselves. **Chapter 3** covers many of my questions, tools, and techniques to help clients express their value-added in order to develop their resume, LinkedIn profile, and interviews.

Chapter 4 and 5 will walk you through how to take the information from chapters 1-3 and use it to create an online presence, such as via LinkedIn, for the main purpose of building relationships. Networking, i.e. relationship building, is where most people are going to find their next job. It's probably where they found their last job too. But how you do this in the online world we live in has changed the game.

I feel so strongly about "honoring all career pathways" in our work that I have given this concept its own spotlight in **Chapter 6.** We have a lot of work to do to ensure people are choosing career pathways that best fit their needs and goals—not someone else's or as a result of societal pressures.

Chapter 7 could have been an entire book on its own—the importance of the conversation between you and your clients. One of my subheadings says it well, "Talk less, nudge more." Whether you use assessments like card sorts or the Strong Inventory, it really is all about the conversation of the results and what they mean to the person.

Chapter 8 and 9 are about you. I believe that if you want to be the best career coach you can be, you must take care of yourself both professionally and personally. These two chapters speak to my belief that we must constantly be learning, and that we need to take care of ourselves so that we can then support and assist our clients.

I get so many questions about starting a private practice and have had great interest in any conference presentations or articles I've written on this topic that I felt a need to add some tips on starting your own private practice in **Chapter 10.**

There are two overriding principles in my philosophy of career development. One is the aforementioned concept of "intentional serendipity"—taking **action** and be open to **discovering something by accident**. I believe we all need to embrace chance events and to even create them by taking action and getting out of our comfort zone. Chance events happen all the time in our lives. Why not look for them and then decide if you want to veer from your set path?

My own career journey is testament to the idea of intentional serendipity. How else does a person go from forestry major, to Director of Student Activities, to the Office of Tourism for the State of Maine, to school counselor, to director of an advising and career center, and eventually to entrepreneur? Luck. Chance events. People who provided support, advice, or opportunity. And then me being willing to change directions and take advantage of those opportunities.

When I work with students or clients I always start off with my philosophy of intentional serendipity. Those nine syllables get their attention. And when I explain what it means, they get it. They don't always *do* it, but most of them "get it."

Mixed into this thinking is my belief that people are not undecided. When a person tells me they are undecided I say, "No you're not. You know what you don't want to do, right?" They nearly always say yes. "So, if you know what you don't want to do, then somewhere down deep you know what you do want to do. Now we just need to go find it." And then the hard work begins.

Throughout the book, I will use the term "career coach" or "career practitioner" to include anyone who provides career services to others—career counselor, academic advisor, facilitator, career development specialist, career advisor, career transitions specialist, etc., also fit. There are so many people providing career services in so many different industries, companies, and organizations. What we all have in common is the desire to help others navigate their own career development.

My goal in writing this book is to help you, the career practitioner, improve what you do to help others navigate their career development. I hope that it will inspire you to take action and continue to learn how to improve your services to your clients/students. When each of us works to improve, we raise our entire career development profession.

Note: The names and identities of people in my "Coaching in Action" sidebars have all been changed to respect the confidentiality of my clients.

CHAPTER 1

Helping Clients Change Their Mindset

"My greatest challenge has been to change the mindset of people. Mindsets play strange tricks on us. We see things the way our minds have instructed our eyes to see."

—Muhammad Yunus

So much of what we do as career coaches is to help people change their mindsets when it comes to career development. All too often people have a very limited scope of what career development is to them—they really have little point of reference other than what they have grown up with, i.e., *I left school and got a job. Now I need to find another one.* (But they have absolutely no idea how to do that.) Or then there's the person who has been laid off from a company they worked at for years and now has to figure out what's next, or the Boomer who had a career in one field but now wants to do "something different" for the next 10 years.

As career coaches we need to help people understand what their career *could* be, and two, that it might be ever-changing. "Career," as defined by the National Career Development Association, is "the combination of activities performed at any given life stage in all roles of life, including the role of worker." When we take this broader definition of "career," it allows us to honor all people for whatever type of skill development they have done—even beyond the traditional workplace scenario.

Take a stay-at-home husband/spouse who volunteers at school, or someone who is unemployed for a long time and volunteers for a local non-profit, or someone who is now attending college or doing some type of long-term training. Learning can happen everywhere in our lives—not just through employment. Helping your clients understand that skill development happens in a variety of roles can then make them look at their roles as parents, children, caretakers, volunteers, and more as skill development. Within these activities, people can also find their passions.

Donald Super was really the first career theorist to look at career development through the eyes of the various roles we play. Super viewed each person in all the roles they take on in life, how their career development is constantly in flux, and how our different roles in life all influence each other. He also really looked at career development as ever-changing over time. After all, we are not the same person at 25 as we are at 55.

For example, my lifestyle and responsibilities while I was a school counselor with a 190-day contract were very different than my time at a community college as the Director of Advising, Career, & Transfer. At the same time, my roles as a parent and spouse were affected by my work roles and time commitments. When I added on duties as the president of the Maine School Counselor Association (MESCA), a volunteer role, my role as a parent and spouse changed once again due to the sometimes long days spent at work or on MESCA responsibilities.

Coaching in Action

Adding a new role (like a new job after being a stay at home mom) can be exciting. But there needs to be a discussion about the realities of new responsibilities and how they affect all the other things going on in a client's life.

I was working with a new community college student who had finally decided to go back to school after raising three children to school age. When her youngest started kindergarten, she decided to start college. Her family was supporting her decision to go back to school.

About half way through the first semester she came to me because she was really struggling in her classes. As we talked, the problem became more evident. Her family still expected her to do the laundry, food shopping, cleaning, and cooking. Her new career as a college student affected all her other roles, and she needed to have a conversation with her husband and children about what could be done to make sure she was successful in her new role.

After talking with her family, she was able to make some progress on changing their expectations of how her new role of being a student again affected her past roles of being a mom and homemaker.

Our job is to help people see their situation from a different perspective. The bigger view. The longer view. Too often people are making decisions based only upon what is directly in front of them right now. When you think back 5-10 years, it is often surprising how much has changed. We can help people envision the future and how their lives will be quite different in 5 or 10 years.

You can help your clients use that "long-view" perspective to make their career decisions today. Asking those good, probing questions that help them see their career development in a broader context is what we do best. So much of what I do is help clients see this big picture and realize that there is space and time in their decisions.

Coaching in Action

I was working with a client, Jane, who was in her mid-50s and had just completed a Medical Assistant associate degree. She was having a difficult time finding work, even though there was a great need for Medical Assistants in our area. She thought it was because of her age. It probably was. So, we discussed what she had been doing that worked and then looked at things that had not worked.

She was being perceived as "old" and possibly "not tech savvy." We began to change **her perspective** on these issues. We worked on getting her resume to "hide" her older dates and highlight her current degree date. We worked on Jane being able to articulate her willingness and ability to figure out new computer software and research on her own until she figures things out. And we stressed that she had a willingness to ask for help if needed.

By changing Jane's perspective of herself and helping her come up with stories that addressed "age" and "lack of tech-savvy" she was able to secure a job within four weeks of our time together.

Not Knowing the Future is Okay

As people head down their own career paths, they all too often cannot _know_ where the journey will go exactly. They can choose a direction, but the actual path appears in a serendipitous manner. We need to help our clients embrace serendipity, **discovering opportunities by accident.** We need to help them be open to possibilities that lie ahead. We can help our clients plan a path and to be open to the possibility that it may not lead to exactly what they thought. It may veer to the right or left, but I *can* say that it will take them somewhere. And that "somewhere" may turn out to be even *better* than the original path.

Help your clients get away from seeing some of these career decisions as "right or wrong" and more as "right or left." We all have many choices to make each day, some are bigger than others. Most people make the best decision they can using the information they have at that time. Each decision will bring different results and at that time you make the best out of the situation. Sometimes "the best" is that you learned something. So, it is not "right or wrong" but simply "right of left".

In August 2012, I backpacked the John Muir Trail/Pacific Crest Trail in California, a 195-mile trip with two great friends. We have now hiked around 1,600 miles of the PCT together over the past 31 years.

As you look at this beautiful picture of the mountains we hiked, **try to find the trail that lies ahead of us.** Every day we looked ahead for the trail and we usually saw something that looked like this picture. Is the trail going to go up this valley to the left? Or is it going to go up and around the far side of that tall peak in the middle? Or will it head into the valley and go right before that peak? Often, we did not know for sure.

Remember to help your clients decide on a direction and to be open to unexpected opportunities.

Action and failure is where the real learning happens
"Failure is success if you learn from it." —Unknown

4 Ways We Can Help Our Clients Move Forward

When people are "stuck," they often need to get out of their comfort zone but are afraid that they will fail. 'Get out of your comfort zone." We've all heard this, but some people think that there is only one zone beyond "comfort" and they call it "panic" or "freak out."

My friend Bryan Murphy, Lead Teacher in the Old Town High School Alternative Education Program, explains to his students that there are actually three zones to think about:

- The **comfort zone,** where no learning takes place. People are complacent here and often go through the motions.
- The **freak out or panic zone,** again, where no learning takes place. When you freak out, you shut down. Not much good is going to happen here.
- But what lies in-between is the key. In between comfort and panic is a zone that Bryan calls the **stretch zone.** This is where learning can happen.

All too often people go from **comfort zone** all the way to **freak out/ panic zone** without slowing down—not collecting $200, not even stopping to eat. If people can identify where they are most comfortable and where they panic, finding something in between is reasonable. How do we get our students/clients to find real learning in that **stretch zone?**

1. Combat fear of failure. One thing we can do is to address the elephant in the room for many people: a fear of failure. Too many people think that failure is only for losers. The reality is that failure is how we learn. Babies fall a lot before they learn to walk. Adults are no different.

We need to help our clients/students embrace failure as a learning opportunity.

2. Action. In order to nudge people out of their **comfort zone** and into that learning zone we are calling the **stretch zone**, people need to take some form of action. Our job is to help people identify action steps that move them out of their **comfort zone** and NOT to their **panic zone.** If a step is too big, they may be overwhelmed. If it's too small, and nothing happens—same old, same old.

Our job as coaches is to help people identify action steps where real learning can take place.

Coaching in Action

I was working with a very experienced I.T. client recently who had been laid off and was desperate to find work here in Maine. He was applying to five or six job boards, searching Craigslist, and applying online…quite comfortable doing this. I told him this was not where he should be spending all his time and effort, as he and 10,000 other people were doing the same thing.

Nudge, nudge. What about the 354 LinkedIn connections you have? How about you call 10 connections a day? That will keep you busy for 30 days.

By moving him into his **stretch zone,** where he picks up the phone and calls people or takes them out for coffee, he will find more results than applying on five or six job boards. As we know, most jobs are in that **hidden job market** and not advertised and your network is the only way to find these jobs.

3. Perspective. As we work with people, the one vital thing we can give them is perspective. They need to know that there is a zone in between **comfort** and **panic**, and that we can help them identify things they can do in that zone to learn. We can let them know they are in a transition, and that everyone goes through transitions in life. According to William Bridges, all transitions have an END (you must accept that something needs to END before you can move on). Each transition has a MIDDLE (where things seem fuzzy, unknown, and uncomfortable). And finally there will be a BEGINNING (where you *will* become something new). Perspective is the one thing I feel really helps many of my clients.

4. Intentional serendipity. Help people understand that chance events are simply a part of life. Being "intentional" means taking action, but then you have to be open to the serendipitous opportunities that come from that action. People need to accept that chance, luck, serendipity, and happenstance are good for us. These areas are where opportunity hides and where real learning happens…outside the **comfort zone.**

Why we all need to "fail forward"

Failing forward is an entrepreneurial philosophy about embracing and learning from failure. Thomas Edison, Wayne Gretzky, Albert Einstein, and Jim Peacock have all had many great failures. The **key is to "fail forward"—learn from your mistakes and don't be afraid to try something new again**

An *Inc.* magazine article talked about a "Failure Church" where one company encourages its employees to proclaim their failures out loud. Some failures are small, some big, and after the person announces their failure, all the attendees applaud wildly! Pretty bizarre, but they all said it feels good to get the failure off their chest and feels even BETTER when their fellow employees applaud. (Read article http://bit.ly/peakcareers105)

Owning up to mistakes actually **encourages employees to try new things**. Too often, we brush failures under the carpet to boast only about our successes, like the gambler who only tells people when they win. But with hard work, perseverance, and some risk-taking, failures often lead to successes. **It is really what you LEARN from the experience that counts.**

Fear of failure can pervade our work life and our personal life—when we don't try something new, nothing new, exciting, or interesting can ever happen. Happenstance Learning Theory tells us we can discover opportunities by taking action and "creating luck," which is the "intentional serendipity" I mentioned before.

A person taking my Facilitating Career Development (FCD) class recently posted how her friend's dad was told he'd never work in the animation field. He was let go by Disney and went on to open a small startup called Pixar. He encouraged his daughter and her friends to always "fail forward": take risks, learn from them, and keep going on to the next thing.

Use "intentional serendipity," take some risks, and remain open to what you discover. College students declare majors and then discover they "don't want to do that," which can be perceived by family and friends as a failure. We need to encourage students to embrace change and to try new things such as info interviews, taking on extracurricular activities, volunteering, internships, etc., and to learn from each activity, even it you learn you do not want to do a job.

Life is not a dress rehearsal. You need to "go for it" when you want to improve your business, better yourself, or help your clients/students learn. Wake up and love what you do as a result of taking chances and enjoying the serendipity that life brings us.

Failure makes me happy

Career learning theory tells us that we can learn by **doing** (*instrumental learning)* or by watching what others do (*associative learning)*. Personally, I've learned the most when I have tried something and failed, like my first Facebook Live event when I told myself to "just do it" and tried to show a PowerPoint, which came out looking like funhouse crazy mirrors. So what? I learned and the next time I tried it, I was better.

As career coaches we need to help our clients move forward by trying new things, taking action steps that may appear to be risky for them. Not knowing if they will be successful but taking action nonetheless. There are no guarantees of success but there is the likelihood you will **learn something in the process** through those actions and sometime failures.

Here are some of my "best failures."

Failure #1

My very creative son has been drawing since he could hold a crayon. At 4 years old he drew a jaw-dropping, multi-sail pirate ship on an Etch-A-Sketch, and in college he majored in Advertising. I had him take every new career assessment I wanted to try out, and he always came up "creative." His suggested lists were all things like graphic design, marketing, desktop publishing, and more creative jobs…just what I expected.

What eventually happened? He took a job as an analyst working with medical electronic records. Hardly creative. I blew that one! Out of the 1,000 occupational titles available, this would have been 985 just above anthropology, aerospace scientist, and electrician for him. Nope, I would never have guessed it as a career counselor or a father.

You know what? **I failed as a career counselor. I never saw it coming.** But happenstance in life takes many forms, and at the end of the day, career counselors should be happy if our clients, students, or children are happy with their occupations. My son is happy. If he is happy, I am happy.

Failure #2

In February 2012 I left a full-time position with benefits as the Director of Advising, Career, and Transfer at our local community college. I thought I would make most of my income in my first year by offering online seminars to career counselors and advisors. I planned to have offered at least three online seminars in the first year. Nope! Other opportunities kept popping up in my life. I ended up working two days a week at a liberal arts college, was asked to keynote a conference, and offered multiple workshops to different agencies.

You know what? **I failed at my prediction** as a business owner. Happenstance once again tricked me—pleasantly, I must admit. I could not have guessed how much I would love being on my own, developing new seminars, taking on new unexpected assignments. I'm happy—delighted might be a better descriptor. Even though I failed to meet my original expectations, I learned a lot, and I look forward to more failures and other unexpected opportunities.

Failures. We all have them. The key is, what did you learn? Failure is what makes us human. It allows us to learn what works and what does not work. Causes us to be creative in how we solve problems. Makes us work together to make a better mousetrap.

When our clients say they "hated that job," or that it was a "bad fit," the key is to ask *why*. That one simple word, "why," is the key to helping people navigate their career paths. *Why* did you think it was a bad fit? What did you like and *why*? And if you feel you "failed," the only real question is, "What did you learn from it?" **We should encourage failing as an educational opportunity.**

So, when you are working with a student or an unemployed person, a person who is confused about what direction to go, **have them evaluate their failures** and look for other places they can fail. Because with enough failures, we often find success. If we know one thing, it's that **doing nothing doesn't work.** Try something, anything, but take action and fail.

Our greatest glory is not in never failing, but in rising every time we fall.
—Confucius (BC 551- 479)

Putting the puzzle pieces together

Career decision-making is like a 1,000-piece puzzle with a number of pieces missing and only a vague picture on the box. Each person thinks they have a complete puzzle to put together. Our job as a career counselor/coach/advisor is to help our clients find as many of the outside pieces as possible to give them the framework and some direction.

Too many people think career decision-making is a linear process, but each person actually takes the puzzle pieces they can find and fits them together to begin to make a picture of themselves. As career practitioners we may use assessments to help fit pieces together, we may use open-ended questions, and we may use work or family history, but ultimately what we are doing is helping the clients/students find pieces that fit together.

What we do is **help people find patterns** in what often appears to be a pile of unrelated puzzle pieces. So many people feel like they are "undecided" or "all over the place," but often we can see themes or patterns. Maybe all of their jobs have been in the REALISTIC Holland type, or maybe they always talk about one specific industry, or maybe they gravitate towards jobs that allow them to work alone and think. Whatever the pattern or theme is, it is often difficult to people to see it themselves.

There are 500 puzzle pieces all over the table. This is going to **require persistence.** My father-in-law loved puzzles, and he would sit for hours and days picking up one piece and trying it in a number of places, sometimes connecting it to another, sometimes setting it down and picking up another piece. Our clients need to remember that discovering their next job may require trying different things over a long period of time. They may need to volunteer, find part-time work, do informational interviews, try a job out for a while, network, and even explore online for information. The hard work comes when you **make the effort to be personal,** like a face-to-face information interview or volunteering.

Occasionally when I work on a puzzle, I just pick up a piece and go with my intuition on where it may fit best. **Career development often requires trusting intuition** and encouraging our clients to "go with their gut." "Does it feel right?" "What if you flipped a coin and it came up heads you take the 'A' job? Does it feel right?" Often the answers are not clear (like our puzzle) and they are not lined up in a sequential, ladder-like process. Sometimes you have to trust and let serendipity take you to a new place. **Maybe the final picture of your puzzle doesn't look like you thought it would.**

Helping our clients see their own career development from a different perspective is so important. "Perception is reality" for everyone, and sometimes people are stuck in their own perception of what their career development looks like. Our job is to help them view their situation from a longer viewpoint, to help them understand that the many roles they play affect each other. We need to let them know that failing is a great learning tool, and that career development is like a puzzle with missing pieces. You'll never have all the pieces, but you can still move forward—especially if you keep in mind that life is full of chance events and opportunities.

Career Coach Tips

- Remember when you are working with clients that they bring their own perspective on the career development process. Check with them and try to understand what their perspective is. Is it optimistic? Is it realistic? Do they know quality career resources? Do they understand the value of networking? Then help them reframe their situation (if needed).
- Encourage "action steps" and a willingness to *discover something by accident* by embracing "intentional serendipity" in their thinking.
- Help clients view obstacles or failures as opportunities to learn.
- Work with your clients to look for themes in their lives and to realize they will never have "all the pieces" of their puzzle. Help them trust their instincts and move forward by taking action.

CHAPTER 2

Create Luck Through Taking Action

"The path to our destination is not always a straight one. We go down the wrong road, we get lost, we turn back. Maybe it doesn't matter which road we embark on. Maybe what matters is that we embark."

—Barbara Hall

When I work with students or clients, I start off with my philosophy of intentional serendipity. Those nine syllables get their attention. And when I explain what it means, "taking action and being open to discovering something by accident," they get it. They don't always DO it, but most of them "get it."

Recently, I was talking to a local businessman and we ended up discussing how people **discover jobs by accident.** His face lit up. "That's exactly what happened to me! In high school, I was thinking about engineering or joining the military and then I discovered machine tool." Thirty years later he was a CEO of a large machine tool company and now is a consultant in that field.

While on my honeymoon, I met the director of a high school technical center. I had no idea what a vocational-technical school was, but four months later, I was working for him and my life was transformed forever with an understanding and appreciation of all kinds of occupations.

We all have stories about chance events that changed the course of our careers. **Then why is it that students and other clients continue to come in and ask to take "one of those assessments that tells me what to do?"** The longer I am in this business, the fewer assessments I use. Our job as career coaches is to help our clients be curious and willing to take some risks: talk to people they don't know, remain open to change, and above all else be willing to change their direction if/when they embrace intentional serendipity and "discover an occupation by accident."

Intentional serendipity is a lens I view from whenever I meet with students or clients. I encourage them to expand their view of the work world, to not get caught looking too narrowly, and to be open to chance events because they are an unavoidable part of life.

In Gregg Levoy's book *Callings*, he devotes a chapter to **synchronicity**—another way to create luck in your search for your new career path. Synchronicity is a meaningful coincidence that can inform us, primarily through intuition. Gregg tells a wonderful story about his frustration with finding work he could be passionate about and when he is at one of his all-time lows, synchronicity enters. He is listening to a song by the Eagles called "Desperado" and as he pulls up to his curb in front of his apartment, he hears the line *"the queen of hearts is always your best friend."* He opens his car door and there on the curb next to his left foot is a playing card: the queen of hearts.

When he mentions this to a friend of his, she says that *when you are on the right path, the universe winks and nods at you from time to time to let you know.* Over the years Gregg found five more queen of hearts playing cards as he continued to search for satisfaction in work. What he came to realize was that he needed to pay attention more to his heart, (less head), more to intuition, (less intellect), and what I call "trusting your instincts".

We want so much to have facts, figures, and data help us decide what to do and sometimes…we need to trust our hunches and pay attention to the signs the universe sends us. Another great story about synchronicity is when my good friend Jordan and his wife Emily were trying to decide if he should take the job offer in Ohio and leave Maine. While on vacation they talked about it and were both struggling with the decision. They were driving in silence for a while and pulled up to a car and the luggage rack on the car had, in big letters, COLUMBUS. The city in Ohio Jordan has his offer. He took the job.

Facts, data, and logic should always be a part of big decisions. But… don't ignore synchronicity, chance, instincts, and your hunches.

Chemist Louis Pasteur said, *"Chance favors the prepared mind."* We should impart this information to our clients. They must be prepared to look for opportunities that can initially appear as obstacles or irrelevant events in their daily life.

Yes, you can create luck and Dr. Richard Wiseman proves it in his book, *The Luck Factor.* (Read my book review here http://bit.ly/peakcareers101).

To do so, the two things you need are to be open to opportunities (see Pasteur's quote above) and to trust your instincts as Greg Levoy points out.

Our instincts have gotten us to this point in humankind after 10,000 years of trying to survive each day. Computers and assessments are helpful, but they're not the only way to move forward in your career search. Trusting your hunches, those instincts that help us navigate our daily lives, are so useful in career searching. You can create luck through taking action, like doing informational interviews, volunteering, or taking a part time job to learn about a field. Doing these types of action steps will give you more information but you must also trust your hunches on what that action might tell you.

Coaching in Action

When I was a school counselor and working with high school students deciding on which college they wanted to attend, I always strongly advised they go on a college tour of the campus. I remember having one senior who was absolutely convinced of her #1 choice… until she went on a campus tour. She came back and said something didn't feel right. She just did not connect with the students there. It was not a specific piece of data or information but a "feeling" that it simply was not a good fit.

Some clients come to me and say they are "undecided" about their career or have no idea what they want to do. Yet most of them **know what they don't want to do.** So, are they really as lost as they think they are? It does not take me long to determine if a person is more "people focused" or more "math/science/structure" focused. All I need to do is ask them if they'd like to do something that is the *opposite* of their personality and they say, "no way."

If a client is not sure what they want to do, the first step is to help them change their mindset. **If you know what you do NOT want to do, then down deep, you must know what you DO want to do.** You just need to find the right words to get a client's head around it and change their way of thinking. Often, they are relieved to hear that maybe they really are not "clueless" about their next steps—they really just need to pay attention to *why* they don't want to do certain types of jobs.

Here are some points to keep in mind when working with undecided clients to help them be open to discovering opportunities.

1. Think skills first, not occupations or job titles

The world we live in today is very different than it was 20 years ago. Employers are looking for a variety of skill sets to increase their production or productivity. If you focus on **skills** and help your clients articulate them to a potential employer, they will have their attention, and might be surprised at the variety of jobs that require those **skills.**

Help your clients think about **past accomplishments** that they are most proud of. What **skills** were they using? **We naturally gravitate to doing things we are good at, and then we do them over again because it feels good.** Pay attention to this and encourage them to trust their hunches (see #3 below). Look for broad skill trends as well as specific skills (e.g., *I am very good at explaining things to groups of people.*).

Ask them, what **classes have they always enjoyed** and why? The "why" question is sometimes harder to answer, but more revealing. Say you enjoyed history classes more than science classes. If so, what is it about history you enjoyed the most? The political ramifications? Cultural changes over time? Getting to know individual people throughout history? The **skill** here might be their ability to analyze broad themes or to analyze and understand people. Think about **what** classes and **why**.

What **jobs did they enjoy** the most, or what parts of jobs did they enjoy the most? Nothing gets us closer to **understanding skills** than using skills. I had two students once that both worked at Dunkin' Donuts—one hated it and the other loved it, both for very different reasons. The reasons are what matter.

Nudge your clients to ask people (like parents, uncles and aunts, close friends, teachers, etc.) what skills they think you have. We fail to ask these questions and assume that we'll figure this out somehow on our own, out of nowhere. I wished I'd asked my dad about my skills when I was in high school. I choose Forestry for a major because I had to pick *something* in my senior year. Turns out a few years ago he told me that as a young child I was always talking to adults and was comfortable talking with all kinds of people, even people I did not know. My skill of helping and communicating with people did not come out until years later to me, but Dad saw it years ago.

2. Encourage them to think about broader industries and types of companies

Don't get too focused on whether they want to work in "graphic design" or "marketing." Think about working in the "creative economy." This will broaden their options and open up many more possibilities they may not be aware of (see #5 below). Are there types of companies that appeal to them more than another, for example, nonprofits vs for-profit?

Are there preferred groupings or industries? Community & Social Services? Healthcare? Media & Communication? Legal? Business & Financial? If so, explore these broader themes on websites such as the Occupational Outlook Handbook. https://www.bls.gov/ooh/

Once they have narrowed this, the next strategic action step is to talk to people who are working in these areas to see what's out there.

Coaching in Action

Remember the game "hot and cold"? Try this. Have your client go to the Occupational Outlook Handbook (OOH) or O*NET https://www.onetonline.org/ (another Dept. of Labor site) websites and simply click on jobs they think they'd like. Then, guide them to look immediately at the link "Similar Occupations" (in OOH) and "Related Occupations" (in ONET). Have them keep clicking on related occupations until they run into a dead end.

Ask them:
• What "feels" right?
• Is there a theme apparent?

When you saw the occupation, do you think, "Am I getting closer here?" (warmer) or, "This is not what I want (colder)."

Guide them to pay attention to that little voice in their head and their gut feeling about jobs because there is an inner voice in all of us that is worth listening to.

When I had a student in my career decision making class do this at the community college, she kept circling back to occupational therapy and occupational therapy assistant (OTA). After looking at our OTA program, she applied and started that program the following year. Before she had played the "related occupations" game, she did not know what occupational therapy was.

3. Trust your instincts

For too long our society has believed that decisions can all be made using logic and/or a quick assessment on a computer. Sorry about that; it's simply not true. I met with a student the other day who had great instincts on what to do. I simply kept saying, *"trust those instincts, you are right on track."* And she was. She just needed to confirm them with me.

Think about it. When you meet people, why is it that some people you immediately like and others you think are kind of creepy? Instincts. It is what has kept humans alive for years. We need to pay attention to them and trust them.

4. Think of yourself as an independent contractor

What I mean is the client must view themselves as a person who **brings a set of skills *to* an employer**. Present themselves as a contractor with a variety of transferable skills they bring to an employer as adding value to their company.

Here's an example: *"I am an excellent writer, have the ability to analyze complex information, synthesize it, and make it understandable to others using my strong writing skills and presentation skills."* When they embrace this thinking, it changes their mindset on what they bring to the table and reinforces the fact they are skilled and can take those skills to a wide variety of employers—not just this position.

Think of this as not looking for a *job* but looking for an opportunity to help an organization make money, save money, or look good.

5. Embrace chance events

We have all had chance events in our lives. Share some of your stories of chance events that demonstrate the non-linear way that life works. Stress the fact that chance events are simply a part of life and should be embraced. Talk about how even though they sometimes look like barriers or hassles, often many positive things happen because of detours from an expected plan.

6. Take action

Moving forward in the job search process requires your clients do something. For many people, success requires doing something ***different*** than they have been doing. The more they go out of their comfort zone, often the better. The obvious detours can include informational interviews, volunteering, taking part-time jobs, or taking a class, but they can be as simple as walking down a different road or driving to an appointment a different way that will expose them to new businesses. **The key is to be intentional in looking for new things that may lead to new opportunities.**

7. Encourage curiosity

Too many people say "I can't just call up someone I don't know and ask them to talk to them. I wouldn't even know what to ask!" We need to help people be curious. It's amazing to me that students will come in and ask me all kinds of questions and they've often never met me before, but when I suggest they speak to a person in the field they want to enter, they get nervous. So, I ask them:

- What is it that you do *not* know about the occupation you are exploring?
- What is it that you really want to know?
- How can you learn more about it?
- Who can you ask?

Then I explain that I am a generalist, and that in order to learn the answers to these questions, they will need to talk to people in the field, or close to the field, or follow targeted discussions in LinkedIn, or ... do *something* else. **But they have to get as close as they can to the field** and searching on websites does not get anyone close enough.

How to help your clients create luck through *action*

Here are some of my go-to action recommendations. Many of these are obvious for most of us in the field but still worth mentioning here.

Informational interviews

These are not just interviews to learn about a specific occupation, but rather interviews to discover **what else is out there**. I encourage my clients to interview a person about an occupation and to ask questions that will help them learn about related occupations, like:

- *What other jobs have you thought about doing that are similar to this?*
- *If you were to do it all over again, would you do something different?*
- *Who else in your company needs these skill sets to be successful?*
- *What was your own career path, and what in your education or training played the greatest role in getting you where you are today?*

By doing informational interviews, your clients are not just looking at that specific job, but also any and all other jobs their interviewee leads them to explore. Clients must create luck by trusting their instincts to discover what else is out there.

More Successful Informational Interview Questions

- Can you describe what a recent day at work was like for you?
- What do you like about your job? What do you dislike?
- How did you get into this field? Is there a specific degree or certification required?
- What are traits and skills that help people be successful in this work?
- What do you see for changes in your industry in the next 5-10 years?
- What advice do you have for me?
- Is there anyone else you can recommend I speak to?

Volunteering

Nudge your client to volunteer in an area that is related to what they are exploring. When they find a place, make sure they do a good job, ask lots of questions, and seek to learn what other people do for work and get their ideas on how their skill sets might be useful in the field. Have your client ask for introductions to someone doing work that interests them.

Part-time job/internships

Part-time jobs and internships are chances to use and develop real skills in a job setting and are great resume builders. Encourage clients to look for opportunities to take on additional tasks and duties while they are there... and do good work. They should also take this opportunity to meet other people in the company and learn what they do. Many times these work experiences can lead to full-time positions.

Researching online

When researching via sites like ONET, Occupational Outlook Handbook, America's Career Infonet, and even LinkedIn, (see chapter 4), clients can let curiosity take them anywhere that looks interesting to create luck and discover something new. On most of the Department of Labor sites noted here, you can search for information using categories or industries or groupings of jobs. Most people don't realize there are many ways to organize jobs. For example, in ONET you can search by career clusters, industries, families, zones, interests, skills, and more. Help your clients explore the world of work in different ways because one way might make more sense to them.

What are the themes? What types of jobs did they find? What do they have in common?

Lead your clients to trust their instincts and go wherever they want to go, letting that serendipity help create luck in finding a potential new job. What I like about this activity is I can literally watch what clients are thinking. Are they gravitating toward a certain industry or skillset? Are they avoiding others?

Reading

Many of my clients don't read much except online, but I encourage them to read anything from blogs, newspapers, magazines, LinkedIn posts — and pay attention to what grabs their attention. Is it "heartfelt stories?" Science? Psychology? I then suggest writing down what they learn or notice in a career journal.

Case in point: A client I was working with had a 20-year background in paralegal work and had moved recently to central Maine. I sensed she was not really interested in continuing to work in the legal world, and we discussed a number of options. **One piece of advice I gave was to follow her instincts and do something she loved to do.** She was offered three jobs: two in the legal field and one as an entry-level position at the Humane Society as a "cat tech." She took that one because she was "excited about it." After a very short period of time, she was offered the Program Director position.

So, was this luck? I say yes, and she created it.

She created it by *trusting her instincts, trying a job that she was excited about, and being open to opportunities that were presented to her.*

Changing Perspectives Using Intentional Serendipity

Let's talk about what else you can do as a career advisor to assist people in "intentionally" creating "serendipitous" events that will lead to opportunity by **changing their perspective of the situation.**

The gift of reframing

One "gift" we have as career advisors is the ability to reframe events in people's lives in such a way to make it look like an opportunity.

People bring us their views of unplanned events or surprises in their lives that, all too often, are framed as obstacles. Our job is to help **reframe these events** and to encourage them to look at them as **career opportunities.**

In an article I wrote for the National Academic Advising Association (NACADA), titled *Academic Advisors And The Wizard of Oz*, I wrote about how the Wizard of Oz did not give them a brain, courage, or a heart, the Scarecrow, Lion, and Tin Man already had those traits. The Wizard gave them the confidence to recognize them. Academic advisors and other career practitioners do much of the same in our work. We help our clients and students see something in themselves they didn't see before. (Read article here http://bit.ly/12nmpIA).

Getting laid off from a job, changing a major because "it didn't work out," or being rejected are events out of clients' control in most cases. The old school answer "things happen for a reason" is close, but not exactly what people need to hear.

As career advisors we can ask:

- What did you learn from this?
- How can you look at this in a positive light?
- What can you do next time?
- Have you ever thought about focusing on your strengths and considering a different or slightly different path?
- Are there other positions at this company that looked interesting?
- If you can't do your initial major, what attracted you to it in the first place? Are there other majors that share those same traits?

Taking these events and encouraging people to look at them differently is the first step in helping them view unexpected events as opportunity.

Perceived barriers vs. real barriers

In order to create "intentional serendipitous opportunities," we need to help people overcome barriers. Some of those barriers are real—no transportation, no internet service, lack of specific skills—but often people create barriers when none exist.

When students say, "I can't possibly call alumni up and ask for an informational interview" or "I can't apply to that position, they are asking for 2 years' experience," we can change the conversation to **creating opportunities** by taking action and breaking down their thinking into parts.

Career advisors can ask:

- What would happen if you *did* call alumni? You came to see *me* today and you didn't know me before, why do you think you can't call the alum?

- Would you like to practice contacting people for information? If so, try these four questions with one of the faculty in your department that you don't know well.
- What would happen if you applied for the position and they viewed your volunteer experience and sports involvement as "experience"?
- What if all the other candidates are not good fits to the company? What if *you* are a great fit for their company? If you don't apply, you'll never know. What is the downside to applying?

**I have found that MOST people have more
perceived barriers than real ones.**

Eeyore is here, now what?

One of the most difficult personality types to work with when trying to create opportunities are the pessimists out there. Why? Because they view everything as a barrier. What these folks really need are three things, **persistence, risk-taking, and flexibility.**

Too often people simply give up too quickly. They may need help in being **persistent.** After grad school, I applied to well over 50 jobs before Colby College hired me. I taped *all* of my rejection letters on my bedroom door. My roommate could not figure out why the heck I would do that! I said, something *will* happen, and I don't want to forget all the hard work I put into this. We need to encourage people to keep going even in the face of repeated denials or dead ends.

Taking **action** is required in order to create opportunity. Many people are averse to risk-taking, and we need to help them move outside their comfort zones and step into the unknown. (Or, at least, a little bit into it.) Some people will need to step slowly, like my previous example of meeting with a faculty member before contacting alumni for career information. When you **take a risk, you create new opportunity**—that is a great lesson for people to learn.

Fostering flexibility

Finally, we can help people be **flexible**. All too often people get set in their ways. They've spent years telling everyone, "I am going to be a _____," then they major in that for three years, and when they realize it won't happen they don't know how to save face.

Our job is to help people reframe this change of plans as a new opportunity. Here are some good questions to ask:

- How can you reframe this change you've made in a positive light?
- What if you said, "I've changed my major from _____ and am now exploring ways to use the following skills in a different field"?

Explain to the student (in this scenario) that **they are not *undecided*,** they have simply eliminated one major. Now they need to focus on what skills they want to use in the next job, and then tell everyone they know their new desired path. The same can be said for adult clients who feel undecided and have tried various occupations.

I talk about **related occupations** all the time. If they liked their first major, there must have been a reason. Now let's figure *why* they liked it or why they *dis*liked it, and work at identifying related occupations that play to their strengths.

Coaching in Action

Here's a concrete example of how you can help clients create their own luck and serendipity. I had a client, Betty, who was working in higher education doing things like recruiting faculty and civic engagement. Her position was ending and she wanted to explore options outside of higher education. We worked on her value-added statement, and then her resume and LinkedIn profiles to reflect this statement. Then she started the process of reaching out for **strategic conversations** with a variety of people.

Strategic conversations are different than informational interviews, where you are looking for specific information about an occupation. In strategic conversations you talk to people who have perspective on an industry or experience working for different companies. You describe to them your value-added to companies and ask for ideas of what to explore next and any other advice they have for you.

A friend of Betty introduced her to a person who worked at a workforce development organization that helped grow jobs for environmentally sustainable enterprises. Betty thought there might be opportunity at this organization. What she discovered in her strategic conversation was two other companies that looked very interesting. She asked for an introduction to people at both companies, and five months later she was the director at one of the non-profits.

Career Coach Tips

- When working with your client, ask them to describe a chance event that happened in their life, say, a person who introduced them to someone who hired them, or an article in the paper that exposed them to a new type of work. Anything! Everyone has chance events in their lives. Help normalize this. If it happened in the past and you got results, then expect it to happen again.
- Help your clients understand that the career development process is often not linear. Even when it appears linear (e.g., person graduates with a Banking major and goes on to work in banking, moving up the ladder) there will be serendipitous events that happen along the way to create opportunities.
- Encourage your clients to take action, any action. It could be informational interviews, strategic conversations, volunteering, anything that gets them to meet people and be exposed to new jobs. And then to be open to discovering something by accident.

CHAPTER 3

Articulating Skills, Values, and Passions

"Through my education, I didn't just develop skills, I didn't just develop the ability to learn, but I developed confidence."

—Michelle Obama

"Focus on something that you have a passion for and hone that skill; it will make you feel confident about your ability."

—Victoria Justice

I believe the core of our work as career coaches/counselors is to help our clients articulate their skills. This is an essential foundation for the career development process. The world of work has many occupations, with more popping up every day. But the *title* of an occupation is not nearly as important as the *skills required to do the job*. For example, if I have strong writing skills, I could be successful writing science or medical books, novels, newsletters or blog posts for a company, or website content for a non-profit, etc. It really is all about the skills first; then comes the occupation title, whatever it may be.

The most important thing our clients should be able to do is articulate their skills and value added to a company. Working with clients, I typically begin with helping them identify their skills. Where I think this starts is working to tap into what is **"authentic," in order to recognize their true selves.** This helps clients identify skills, but also much more than that.

Being authentic is finding the core of who we are. This doesn't change as we get older; it should only get clearer. Although I have had a number of different jobs over the years, there are two themes that continue to show themselves. In nearly every job I have had, I was focused on the "development" of people: student development in my higher education jobs, personal and career development for high school students and community college students, and professional development for career coaches. This is what drives me. It's why I get up in the morning, and it keeps my creative juices flowing. The second authentic theme is my writing, as evidenced by my weekly emails, blogs, newsletters, and even a Christmas newsletter that I have sent out for over 30 years now. Help your clients discover their themes and then build on them.

Coaching in Action- Finding the Authentic Person

We need to find our strengths and build upon them. **Finding the authentic person inside ourselves and our clients takes time and effort.**

I encourage you to watch this YouTube video by Marcus Buckingham, The Truth About You (23 minutes you will not regret). Watch at http://bit.ly/peakcareers106 In it, he explores this topic in a very provocative way and makes a powerful message about finding strengths and discovering the real you, and details why that is so important in careers where we typically spend more than 2,000 hours each year.

Carol Vechio, Life Design & Career Counselor, International Speaker, Author wrote an article titled "Working Toward Achieving Life-Career Satisfaction" in the National Career Development Association's *Career Developments* Fall 2013 magazine that speaks to finding your "True Self" as a way of discovering purpose. True Self is the essence of who you really are and asks the question, "What is my purpose in life?" or "What would a meaningful life look like to me?" **Discovering this True Self requires intense active listening to your feelings, plus a bit of intuition—both from the clients themselves and also from career practitioners when working with clients.**

Vechio challenges us to redefine success in our lives. As Ralph Waldo Emerson said, "Success comes from within, not from without." Finding career satisfaction requires introspection and redefinition of what values are important to your clients—all steps closer to identifying strengths, values, and passions. Trusting instincts is something I talk about with all my clients. **Far too many people want to believe that the answer is in an assessment or a computer search.** I tell people the answer is within themselves. You need to listen that voice in your head—the instincts within ... your guardian angel.

I am working with a client right now who keeps talking about elements he would like in his next job, such as having "work-life balance" and "moral fulfillment" and "job tranquility." These are his values speaking to him and are a reflection of his unhappiness in his current job, which is missing these traits. These are not *skills* he possesses, but *values* he desires. **Values are what are in our soul and need to be a part of the conversation with our clients and ourselves.**

After a blog post I wrote regarding passion, I heard from Nik Crain, Career Development Specialist for the Peace Corp, who wrote that "purpose" is:

"... what gets you out of bed to go to work' and the answer can be either be 'passion,' which is when there is an alignment with the organization mission— even though they don't love the actual tasks of the job. Or it could be more about their 'skills' and they love the work, even though neutral about organizational mission/product/etc. Either one can feed the soul."

I love this view because too many people are searching first for "passion," and then a job that feeds it. This could happen. But more commonly, instead, we may find "purpose" as the driving force at work and "passion" being something you seek outside of work.

All relationships require a level of trust. **Trust can only be gained by being authentic with each other.** My good friend, Dr. Will Keim often spoke about the "education of character." One of his favorite quotes was, "Say what you mean. Do what you say. And when you don't, admit it." He was greatly influenced by the work of Dr. Martin Buber who said, "Education worthy of the name is essentially the education of character." **Character is where you find the authentic you.**

As I think about this topic of "finding purpose" in our work, I can't help but come back to the first steps of understanding ourselves, our skills, and our values. Have your clients ask themselves: What is important to me? What feeds my soul? What gives me energy? Then, stress the importance of having them aim for authenticity by living those out in everything they do. **By showing their true character and "... saying what they mean, and doing what they say" in work, play, and life, then they will begin to find purpose.**

Articulating Strengths

So how do you help your clients discover their strengths? Help them pay attention to *all* their experiences: at work, at play, and at rest. Which ones give them energy? Which ones leave them tired? Which do they dread? Encourage them to spend their time on the activities that give them energy. Then, rinse and repeat. This is where the authentic person is hiding. Some people need help doing this, and that is where we as career practitioners can come in. I like to use skills card sorts. (See following SIDEBAR). Other times I ask probing questions that help people highlight their strengths.

Four steps to help clients define and articulate their skills

1. Get a baseline

I like to start off with a series of questions to see how well the client can articulate their skills and traits in the workplace. Some people need more "nudging" to get them to think of "skills" first. I may ask follow-up questions to get them to describe the tasks and duties at work and which ones they enjoy. By listening closely to what they say (what words they use, and how they describe things), I can usually pick up on skill sets they take for granted as things that "everyone can do."

Here are some follow-up questions you can ask:
- **What makes you unique in the workplace?** (Think about what others at work might say about you.)
- **What are your top 3-5 skills/ traits/talents at work?** (Are you very creative? Are you able to fix things well? Are you always on time?)
- **What are you passionate about doing?** Think about a time you were in "flow" at work and lost track of time. (Problem-solving? Helping others? Researching?)
- **What do you do well?** (Think about work, hobbies, school, and volunteer experience.)

Note: If people are really struggling with this, I will often have them do a skills card sort, which helps them identify specific skills and lets them organize those skills in various ways. I find this can be very empowering for them.

Coaching in Action - Using a Skills Card Sort

I use both the Knowdell's Motivational Skills card sort and SkillScan. I have the clients sort the skills they love to use and then by their level of competence. This is what Dick Knowdell calls the 'motivational skills' piece. Because if you love to use certain skills and you are good at using them, find ways to use them more often and you'll be happy.

What I do then is have the clients take their top skills noted above and "sort them into groups or themes that make sense to you." Because they have already touched each card at least twice, they have already begun to process what that means to them. Once they have their groups we discuss what each group is and examples of how they have demonstrated those groups in their current job or past positions.

I love using card sorts as a way to get my clients thinking about skills, passions, interests, strengths, and values, and then begin to think about prioritizing and connecting the dots between these various areas. **The cards are a kinesthetic way of getting their heads away from the idea that they're looking for an** *occupation.* It allows them to really look at what is truly important to them, and to consider what they bring to the table. The process will then generate discussion and greater thinking.

2. Ask them to tell you a story

The next step is to ask clients to **tell you a story about an accomplishment they are proud of,** or to describe a time they were most happy in their career or volunteer work (even in a part-time jobs when they were young). It's often good to ask a few questions worded a little differently in order to get them to think about the scenario in different ways. **What I listen for here are what skill they used and how passionate they sound describing the situation.** Are there values being described? What actual *words* are they using?

I nudge them to answer this question in the **SAR method** (although I don't tell them, I just guide them through questions).

> S: Describe the SITUATION.
> A: What ACTION steps did they take? (i.e. what skills were used/
>   what traits were highlighted)
> R: What RESULTS came about?

I find that by telling me a story or describing something they did, clients' true skills and traits come out. I ask them what skills were involved and then help them uncover even more skills based upon their story. I am also listening for specific words they use and even a phrase they may say that can then be used on their resume or LinkedIn profile.

Coaching in Action

A recent client of mine, Judy, told me one of her accomplishments was setting up a large event in Boston to celebrate a great year for her company. Her main role is as a purchasing buyer, but she took on this responsibility when asked and loved it.

She was responsible for contacting the hotel and setting up all aspects of the day-long event that included an overnight at the hotel for families. (Multi-tasking skills/communication skills).

She also needed to communicate with the supervisors in her company and a committee of people to ensure that the various events were going to work out the way they wanted them to. (Communication skills, listening, working with a variety of people)

The event went off without a problem, her supervisors were extremely happy with her abilities and follow through, and her colleagues were very appreciative.

As we discussed her accomplishment story, we were able to pull out her skills, and even more importantly, her motivation when planning the event—to recognize her fellow workers in a positive way. Her current job as purchasing buyer was not "feeding" any of her skills and passions that she wanted to build upon.

When your clients tell you stories, you will often hear nuggets that can be helpful in better understanding them. One nugget I heard in Judy's story was people responding to her with comments like, "If Judy gave you the information then it is correct." This demonstrated her work is always well thought out and detail-oriented. Lots of people do not want to brag, but when they are telling a story these tidbits will spill out. Pay attention and follow up on these details.

3. Create value

The next step is to get the client to develop a value-added statement that describes their skills, traits, and interests in a way that clearly shows what they bring to the workplace. This begins with a recap of the main skills and traits they have talked about—I usually have them bullet these out first. Then, they can turn these bullets into a paragraph or two that speaks in their own authentic "voice."

Once they capture the essence of their skills and traits, you can have them add the answers to questions like, "What type of company do you want to work for?" or "What type of industry do you want to work in? Help your clients add anything that gives a clue as to where they want to go.

Here is an example of a value-added statement from one of my clients:

"A Senior Multimedia Professional with 10 years of experience in video production, marketing, and corporate communications. Exceeding expectations for clients in corporate, educational, industrial, and legal settings is my mission. Effective, compelling, and modern storytelling through words and images is the means. Looking for opportunities to become a valued contributor with a mid-sized or larger organization in the Greater Portland, Maine region."

4. Now the process begins

Once your clients have a clear value-added statement, this becomes **the core of everything they do** in the career development process of looking for work.

Here are my usual next steps:

1. We work together to **create a resume** that reflects and highlights this statement, by working it into a Summary statement at the top of their resume and re-ordering bullets in their Experience sections.

2. On LinkedIn, we **create a Summary statement** in their profile.

3. We work language from their statement into the **cover letter**.

4. When clients network with others, I advise them on how to use this statement **to introduce themselves**.

5. When prepping for an interview, I help them **prepare stories** for each skill they want to highlight.

The key is to have the client get the value-added statement in their heads and then make sure they are getting that same message out across all their platforms and messaging.

Coaching in Action

Here is an example of a client's value-added statement that then became the top of her resume. You can see there is a lot of information here. Not only did we get in the fact that she is a project manager, but we also stressed that her motivation is all about developing team members.

We then used this same information in her LinkedIn profile using the header "Long Term Multi-Layered Project Manager Who Thrives to Develop Team Members." Her LinkedIn Summary section then builds on each bullet with a paragraph that demonstrates specific accomplishments.

Note: The line "…who thrives to develop team members" was a line she said when I asked her to talk about one of her card sorts groups and to give me an example. Always be listening to their words and phrases.

Susan Reebok
sreebok1234@ gmail.com ★ 207-666-6666 ★ LinkedIn/susanreebok

Long Term Multi-Layered Project Manager Who Thrives to Develop Team Members

PROFESSIONAL SUMMARY

♦ Demonstrated success working on long term projects, both domestically and internationally, with successful involvement in each aspect from conception through to completion.
♦ Proven ability to build and maintain successful relationships while developing team members.
♦ Maintained a high level of focus while working on multiple large-scale projects simultaneously.
♦ Excellent presentation and public speaking skills; provided content for freelance employees to high-level executives.

I am working with a number of clients right now who struggle to define what skills they bring to the workplace. Our work together is focused on really mining out **what they do** and **what makes them unique**. In other words, **what value do they add to the workplace?**

For example, after three meetings with one client, he was able to create this value-added statement.

> *I have the ability to find solutions for complex problems by utilizing my work experiences and skills. I enjoy the personal satisfaction of keeping customers happy by fixing problems quickly and maintaining equipment to prevent outages. In doing this I have helped maintain a professional reliable reputation, with customer service being at the highest priority. I would like to work for a company where I can transition my skills to work in other electronic fields, communications, or cellular areas where that same dedication to critical messaging is at their highest priority.*

Once we had this refined, we were able to develop his resume, cover letter, and LinkedIn profile, and prepare for an interview.

Another example is when I was working with a college student who felt lost and uncertain about where she was heading. I first had her do a skills card sort that helped her identify and group her top skills into themes. After seeing her skills on the table, she could see her themes and began to articulate what was important to her.

Her first draft of her value-added statement looked something like this:

> *I am a senior graduating with an Environmental Studies major interested in combining my understanding of the environment through education in order to make real change. I want to be invited to science / research but not actually do the research and want to be aware of policy development but not actually do it, with the goal to immerse myself in Latin American communities in order to make change.*

By using a skills card sort she was able to visualize her skills, prioritize them, and then talk about what each group meant to her. She was also able to define what she did *not* want to do. Just asking those open-ended questions that allow people to talk, and then actively listening to what they are saying, is so important. People will use the words that are most important to them without even realizing it.

Ask Your Inner Circle for Assistance

Another way for clients to identify their top skills and traits is to ask people. Have them ask 10-20 people who know them well, each from different perspectives (high school/college friends, former coworkers, supervisors, relatives, etc.), what they see as their top skills and traits.

For example, recently I identified five people close to me who know me very well. I asked them to identify my top three skills and what makes me unique in the workplace. Many of them said I was knowledgeable about my field, very approachable, friendly and genuine, and that I relate to a variety of people. They saw me as a great communicator with a positive attitude. They also said I was someone who gladly shares knowledge and is passionate about the career field.

From the folks who got back to me, and from my own vision of myself, here's what I came up with for my value-added statement:

One of my greatest strengths is the ability to engage people and take big ideas and make them practical. (It's probably the tradesmen on my mother's side that have given me this practical approach. Her family consisted of masons, electricians, cabinet makers, and carpenters.)

I have built my business on the principle that I "want to do the greatest good for the greatest number of people." I decided long ago that I love career counseling and coaching, but because I could only meet one student/client at a time, I could affect more lives by offering training to career counselors and coaches.

As your clients go through this process, remember that <u>today is not the day to be humble</u>. (Read blog http://bit.ly/peakcareers107) Help them identify skills, strengths, passions, and values—and then articulate them to others. Help them understand they are not bragging, they're just describing what they do best. Remember, the goal is for the client to articulate their value they can add to a company and either land a job or discover one that fits them best.

Skills can be developed a wide variety of ways—through on-the-job training, short-term certificates or diplomas, online through YouTube or Lynda.com, as well as by earning a college degree. Our economy needs *all* kinds of skills to run. Challenge yourself to look for and honor all training options and occupations in your work.

Mid-life Career Changers

How do you find that "sweet spot" when working with career changers? Well, my advice is no different than what I often discuss with college students; ask them, "What do you bring to the company or organization that you want to work for?"

The biggest difference for career changers is that they have an opportunity to look back on their years of experience with deeper knowledge and perspective. Whether they want to leave jobs they've held for many years or find new, meaningful activities to do with their 40 hours per week, most of them still want to somehow make an impact.

Our role as career coaches or practitioners is to open up discussions to help people find that "'sweet spot,'" and to **help them identify and articulate the key pieces** that are most important to them.

As stated earlier, I love using card sorts as a way to get my clients thinking about skills, passions, interests, strengths, and/or values, and then to begin thinking about prioritizing and connecting the dots between these various areas. My clients often have trouble articulating what they're good at and what they want. The cards help prompt their thinking.

In my "Working with Boomers to Reinvent Retirement" online seminar, we have used cards to look at passions, strengths, and concerns. We've also used an online assessment that helps people determine what values they want to focus on in the near future. When working with passions, I like to explore if a client has a passion they've always wanted to pursue but didn't because their job got in the way. Is there a new passion they discovered by chance in their own career development, through their social connections, or even just through curiosity? **The questions to ask people are** *"What are you passionate about? How can you explore it more deeply?"*

When we examine strengths using the cards, the challenge is to look beyond the top strengths that clients have developed in their current job. The objective is to also explore some skills that may have been untapped in their work they could bring to a new company or organization.

The values discussion is often interesting, as the assessment I use online does not rate which values are important to the client, but rather **which ones need attention right now.** Most people know what is important to them at some level, but the active discussion should be about where clients are going to put their energy *now* in order to focus on their values. One client I work with wanted to do something to contribute to his local community but didn't want to be tied to a specific time each week or day. What we discovered was that by raising his chickens, collecting eggs, and donating them to the local food pantry, he was using his time the way he wanted but was still able to contribute to his local community in a positive way.

I've found that by spending **one week on strengths, another week on passions or interest, and one more week on values,** my clients then have a chance to process and think about each of these elements separately. Then our work begins to connect these different areas to find that "sweet spot" for their next move, whether it's paid or volunteer. Remember—you might be the first person to ask these questions and to initiate discussions that are thought-provoking for your clients.

Brain research has proven we should give a few action steps (what I call homework) for our clients that can be accomplished in 2–5 days. This gives clients a feeling of moving forward and making progress in their career development. I also find it reinforces the idea that this is a process, and therefore requires a lot of thinking.

So, when working with clients keep in mind that whatever their next move is, it is likely to involve trying to find that "sweet spot" that encompasses passions, strengths, and values. This is where much of the thinking happens. Our job as coaches is to help clients find words that mean something to them, and then to help them find ways to group these words together in meaningful ways that bring forth a life plan.

Career Coach Tips

- The most important thing our clients can do is to be able to articulate their skills and value-added to a company.
- Ask open-ended questions to get the client to talk ... and think. They may not even be able to answer your questions in the session, but they will think about them. Then, maybe next time you get together, you will see progress.
- Listen to the client first. Work hard to be the person talking the least. The client should be talking and thinking. **Clients will say the words that are most important to them.** Really listen to what they say and the exact words being used. Those are clues for you.
- Help the client identify the 5 or 6 essential things (skills, traits, industries, values, etc.) that they want everyone to know about them. Then make sure they weave that into their resume, LinkedIn profile, cover letters, conversations, and interviews.

CHAPTER 4

Sending Your Message on LinkedIn

"...when used correctly, and with panache, LinkedIn can perform near miracles for your career's development. Recruiters and employers both use LinkedIn to source candidates for employment, sometimes using recently departed employees or newly placed employees for career-networking opportunities of their own."

—Alison Doyle, Job Search Expert for The Balance

At minimum, everyone should have a professional online presence. For most of my clients I suggest letting Facebook, Instagram, and other platforms take care of your personal life and LinkedIn be your professional presence.

This is not to say that Twitter, Facebook, Instagram, and other social media platforms do not have a role to play in career development. "It depends" is the answer. It depends on the industry, career goals, and where your audience spends their time. You will need to choose which platform is best for your clients. My point in this chapter is that LinkedIn is the one social media site whose purpose is professional networking—it is the largest career database in the world.

When people search for your clients because they have applied for a position in their company, what will they find?

When people search for anyone on the internet, their LinkedIn profile will typically be at the top of the list, above Facebook and other social media platforms. Why not train your clients to have the **5-6 essential things they want everyone to know about them right there**, front and center? Ask your clients: Will potential employers see your skills and value on your LinkedIn profile? Will they see it on your other social media platforms? (If not, you may want to advise your clients to enable more restrictive privacy settings on Facebook, Instagram etc., if they do not help portray a professional image.)

Top 25 Industries on LinkedIn

1	Information Technology & Services	17,076,099
2	Hospital & Health Care	13,445,850
3	Construction	12,878,172
4	Education Management	10,294,354
5	Retail	10,289,983
6	Financial Services	9,450,549
7	Accounting	8,527,864
8	Computer Software	7,938,087
9	Automotive	7,708,673
10	Government Administration	7,486,477
11	Banking	7,472,071
12	Marketing and Advertising	7,447,442
13	Higher Education	7,392,617
14	Health, Wellness & Fitness	6,599,303
15	Real Estate	6,384,135
16	Telecommunications	6,263,932
17	Oil & Energy	5,986,554
18	Food & Beverages	5,805,185
19	Mechanical or Industrial Engineering	5,257,926
20	Hospitality	5,095,957
21	Electrical & Electronic Manufacturing	4,894,985
22	Insurance	4,884,242
23	Primary/Secondary Education	4,774,434
24	Human Resources	4,408,289
25	Internet	4,400,270

Your clients need to know they *will* be looked at online—if they choose to ignore this area they could get burned. I was working with a very qualified client who was hoping to reduce his commute of 70 miles to less than 20. He could not understand why he wasn't getting any interviews. I think his reluctance to be on LinkedIn hurt him because not only

LinkedIn: To Be or Not To Be

As career professionals, we recognize the importance of networking and finding quality information to research companies, people, and trends. LinkedIn is the largest career database in the world, so we need to be familiar with it in order to properly do our jobs. However not all of our clients need to be on LinkedIn as some occupations are not represented very well on the platform.

A basic summary: LinkedIn is a great tool for most people in professional positions but is not as valuable for those working in some industries. More specifically, the 10 least-represented industries on LinkedIn are shipbuilding, think tanks, political organizations, fishery, fundraising, tobacco, railroad manufacturing, alternative dispute resolution, nanotechnology, and legislative offices.

Is this a reflection of the numbers of people who work in the field?

Or are these just industries that don't need what LinkedIn offers?

Keep in mind, these numbers aren't meaningless—even the field of nanotechnology has 177,799 (as of February 17, 2019).

I would still consider having a LinkedIn profile in some cases for even the bottom 10 industries, as it can still help you create your professional online presence. Even in these smaller industries, you want people to know you professionally. And 177,799 people in nanotechnology is still a significant community!

I wanted to know what LinkedIn's top industries were but could not find anything more recent than 2016. So, in February 2019, my virtual assistant used the LinkedIn search function to look up every industry on LinkedIn and to note how many people were represented.

For clients interested in occupations with strong LinkedIn representation, we need to do our best to assist them in creating strong profiles and understanding how to utilize the many benefits of the platform.

If you'd like to see the entire list go to:
http://bit.ly/peakcareers103

was his profile not complete, his presence on LinkedIn was non-existent. I helped him improve his LinkedIn profile, but he did not really accept the idea his LinkedIn presence could affect the way people saw him as a candidate. (I am happy to say after working with him, he did land a job less than 20 miles from his home)

I suspect human resource people were looking him up online and seeing his weak profile. When HR has multiple qualified candidates that all look fairly equal and they check them out online and find a LinkedIn profile that does not match what an applicant is saying on a resume (or it does not have keywords and a value clearly stated), they will lean towards the candidate who *does* have confirmation of what they are looking for.

LinkedIn is your clients' chance to be authentic and to highlight their value-added to a company—any company. It is also an opportunity for them to *prove* they can do things.

So... where should clients start?

LinkedIn—Start from the Beginning

Inigo Montoya in *The Princess Bride* (my favorite all-time movie) said, "I am waiting for you, Vizzini! You told me to go back to the beginning... so I have."

With over 600 million people on LinkedIn (as of March 2019) and most of them in professional positions, **to be current you (and your clients)** need to learn what LinkedIn is and how to leverage its power.

For many people I work with they really need to "go back to the beginning" and create or update their profile—and know *why* they are doing it.

Why should clients be on LinkedIn? Among many other things, the platform allows you to:
- Create a professional online presence
- Identify and make connections to develop your network
- Identify groups that are discussing topics of interest
- Research companies
- Find employment
- Learn more about your industry

How to create or improve a profile

Because LinkedIn changes over time, I will keep my tips more general in nature here. For the most up to date information and tips on LinkedIn go to http://bit.ly/peakcareers108

Your picture: Your clients should have a professional looking picture, preferably with a blank background (i.e., not taken at the formal dance). Do a quick search for people on LinkedIn and see how their pictures show up for ideas. Aim for not too close, not too far away, and not too busy in the background. You can indeed have a professional picture taken, but it is not necessary in my opinion.

Tagline/Headline: This area immediately under the name is pulled automatically from a section in a user's profile with their most current position. I see this section referred to as "tagline" or "headline" so I am including both here. Work with your clients to edit this section to highlight their career interests, skills, or passions. When people search, they see a user's picture and this tagline, so it is important for your client to capture a highlight of who they are in this section. Check out other people's profiles and generate some ideas on what might work for each specific client.

Example: **Career Coach | Passionate | Creative | Problem Solver**
Example: **Higher Education Professional | Collaborator & Connector**

Summary section: Under a user's name and headline is a blue box with the words "Add Profile Section." Users can click here to add a Summary. Think of this section a bit like a cover letter. This is an area where clients can write about themselves—their strengths, passions, interests, etc. This is the information that you might not find on a resume. Keep it short—bullets work well or short paragraphs—and brainstorm with clients to think of ways to set themselves apart from the other candidates looking for employment. This section should build off the key points already made in the Tagline/Headline.

Customize your LinkedIn address: Users can change their LinkedIn address/ public profile URL and then add it to a resume, business cards, and/or an email signature. On the Profile page, look to the right column for "Edit Your Public Profile."

- In the upper right of that page click on "Edit URL."
- Your client can simply put in their name, or if their name is taken, can use their name with a simple number after it.
- Click "Save" at the bottom.

In our digital-first world, it's important our messaging remains focused and congruent. Congruency of brand and message, especially online, are key to getting found and attracting the right leads and customers. Congruent messaging, especially online, builds trust and authenticity. In my opinion, there's no greater compliment about your online presence than hearing someone say, "you're the same person in real life as you are online."
—Ryan Rhoten Owner, CareerBrand and author of *CareerKred*.

Experience section: This is the one area that will look much like a resume. You can help your clients add a few "bells and whistles" here, but they should start with replicating what they have on their resume. In most cases it is not necessary to put in the months they started and ended a position—just the years is sufficient for most people. An exception to this are college students who are highlighting summer jobs or internships of value.

Skills section: Have your clients take some time and look at people's profiles who are working in the industry/occupation that interests them. They should check out the "Skills" listed and notice if they have those same skills—if so, they can add them to their own Skills section. When filling out this section, clients should think about the top skills employers are looking for—this is one of the sections recruiters use to search for candidates.

Once you have helped your client get their LinkedIn profile in pretty good shape, you both can then focus on "What the heck happens now?"

LinkedIn is a Toolbox

Everyone has their own career development path. Your potential clients are either looking for work or they will be. Even if they retire, it is likely they will be looking for ideas on where to spend their time and energy.

Here are some tips on how they can use the LinkedIn toolbox.

To build personal relationships

LinkedIn is a tool that can be used to develop relationships with other professionals. Career development is all personal—it is not often that someone gets hired from a text or an email they receive.

- **Tip: I advise clients to stay focused on the people that matter to them when building their network.** Just as you would if you were face-to-face. You do not have to accept everyone who asks you to connect, there are spammers out there and others who just want access to your network. And when you do request to connect with someone on LinkedIn, always add an individualized note of request.
- **Tip: Clients should use LinkedIn to seek advice, meet others, and help others on their career paths.** They should aim to make it personal by reaching out to people in their network occasionally and trying to take the relationship from the virtual world to the real world.

To research

LinkedIn is one of the many tools out there to research a company to see what is going on *inside*. What is the company writing about? Who works there now? Who worked there previously?

- **Tip: Help clients use LinkedIn to identify as much as they can about a company.** Do they have any 1st or 2nd connections who could give them insight? Are there any groups related to the company or industry they could follow or join?

To identify career paths

Clients should use LinkedIn to identify people who are doing what they'd like to do and check out their path. How did they get to where they are? The answer will probably be surprising.

- **Tip:** Clients should go to their Alumni page (search for their college or university and find the ALUMNI link- currently on the left side of the college or university landing page) to **look up alumni who majored in their same major and check out their career paths.** Where did they start? How long were they there? Are there paths your client has not thought about?

SENDING YOUR MESSAGE ON LINKEDIN

To reach out the old-fashioned way

LinkedIn is a tool clients should use to discover new career paths, meet new people, learn from others in groups, and develop personal and professional relationships.

- **Tip:** Clients can use LinkedIn to identify people who might be helpful to them. **Then look up their company online,** call the company, and ask to speak to that person. Yes, old-school phone call. They can just go all "Neanderthal" and call them on the phone, making it personal. There will be time later to connect and message through LinkedIn after a phone call.

- I do not recommend sending messages on LinkedIn unless you **know** the person is active on LinkedIn. Use my above tip and call first or email them (if you can find their email on the company website or in their LinkedIn profile).

- LinkedIn is NOT the end result. Finding a job on LinkedIn is a slower process. **It is a tool that will help your clients learn about their desired industries and develop relationships** (online and hopefully in person) that will help them along their career development paths.

> 94% of hiring managers use LinkedIn for recruiting

Backing up your LinkedIn Profile and Contacts

Note: LinkedIn makes changes all the time and I run the risk here of explaining how to do things and by the time you read the book they could have changed. For example, when I was writing the book in the fall of 2018, you could backup your contacts and you would receive their emails. In my final draft, my good friend Sabrina Woods, LinkedIn trainer, pointed out that LinkedIn does not give you emails anymore.

There is quite a bit of work that goes into building a LinkedIn profile and expanding contacts over time. Remind your clients that they should protect their investment of time. I know of people who have been locked out of their LinkedIn profiles or ... their profiles simply disappeared! My heart just started beating faster as I wrote that.

I have been on LinkedIn since 2007 and have seen many updates and changes over those years. I also have about 1,500 contacts I have worked hard to get. **I'd hate to lose my profile information and contacts.**

Every 6 months I back up my profile and contacts. I suggest you, and your clients do this too—no one wants to lose all this hard work they've put in. As of early 2019, this is what you do:

Go to SETTINGS & PRIVACY

Scroll down to DOWNLOAD YOUR DATA

Select PROFILE and CONTACTS (names only, not emails)

They will email you the files, typically within 24 hours.

When you request your profile backup, it will be in PDF format which means the information still has to be typed it back in, but at least the content and wording you created is there to look at and copy. Your contacts are sent to you in spreadsheet format (cvs).

If you follow me on LinkedIn, I send out reminders every 6 months with the current steps on how to back up your profile. For the current method in backing up your profile, go to http://bit.ly/peakcareers109

Career Coach Tips

- LinkedIn is the largest career database in the world with tons of content. For people working in career development, it is an important tool in your toolbox. For your clients it can be very helpful in finding that next job.
- 90% of people already have an online presence. LinkedIn is one key place that clients can use to create a professional online presence.
- Networking is an important component of career development (see chapter 5) and LinkedIn is a great way to build professional relationships and networks.

Because there is so much information on LinkedIn and there are so many changes happening all the time, you can find my current blogs on LinkedIn at http://bit.ly/peakcareers108

CHAPTER 5

Why Networking is Relationship Building

Identify on LinkedIn, engage on Twitter and seal over coffee.
—Chaim Shapiro, Director Office for Student Success, Touro College

Because 80% of all jobs are not posted, the best way to find out about a job opportunity is to have a strong relationship with as many people as you can. As career coaches it is important that we help our clients understand the importance of building professional relationships every day—not just the times they are looking for work. People "buy" from others they **know, like, and trust**. When I say "buy" this includes "want to help," which is the core of relationship building.

Why does the word "networking" conjure up such negative thoughts for people? **Many of the clients and students I have worked with seem to believe it is only for "professionals" dressed in suits, playing golf, and smoking cigars.** That image is not *my* image of networking. So, I asked myself, "What is the best way for me to explain networking to my clients?"

Personally, I like to describe networking as **"relationship building."** This implies a two-way relationship that requires giving and receiving. Relationships take time, communication, and need to offer value of some sort to both people. Clients need to reach out to people and listen to what their "story" is and then tell their own "story"—either face-to-face or virtually. It is all about developing a relationship through authenticity.

Sometimes it is as simple as sending an email that says, "I haven't heard from you in a while. How are things going? Do you have any recommendations for _____?". Express to clients that everyone they know has the potential to be a part of their network. They should be

51

thoughtful about who adds value to their career, and then work to build those relationships.

Make it Personal

Checking in with people is great, especially if you can personalize it. For example, if I know a person in my network reads a lot, I might ask for book recommendations in the above example. I might also share a recent good book I've read. Remember, networking is a two-way relationship.

People "buy" from others they Know, Like, and Trust.

Occasionally people contact me and want to talk about the career field. When someone contacts me who was referred by a person I **know, like, and trust**, I will nearly always take the time to talk with them. If I get a cold call, it is harder to find time available in my busy day. I have to believe my network will refer quality people to me, which helps me prioritize. By having a viable network of people, your clients and their networks will have access to more information and opportunities.

Networking is often referred to as a "connection," but that word does not feel warm or authentic enough for me. Connections are just that... people I am connected with. **My professional network has a much stronger emotional feel to it, one that I hope is more mutually beneficial**, i.e., *Can I help a person in my network?* Is just as important as, *Can people in my network help me?* You should express to your clients that sometimes they need to do good things, even when nobody's watching, because karma will often reward them later...when they least expect it. Remember, the trait of helping others is something employers look for when hiring.

Part of the problem with a term like "networking" is that it can be defined in different ways depending upon how it is being used. Don Asher, author of *Get Any Job*, suggests that we tell our students, "Networking is simply talking to people." The key point here is that we need to define what networking is for our clients, so they can understand the value of it in the context of their career development—this is why I prefer to call it "building relationships." (Read my review of Don's book http://bit.ly/peakcareers102)

Your Network's Network

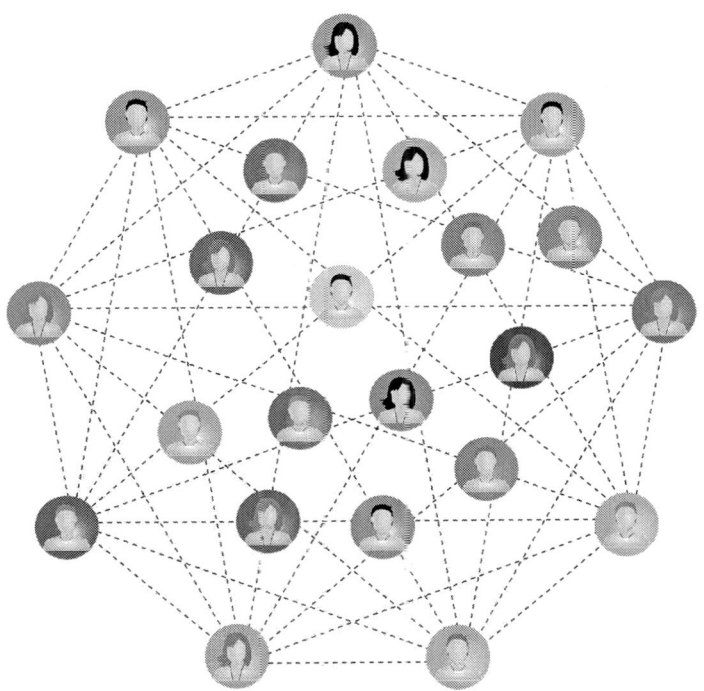

I often talk with my clients/students about how their network is comprised of much more than just first connections. The people who can *really* help you are often your network's network. What LinkedIn calls your "2nd connections."

By having a strong network, people have access to more information, opportunities, and chances of discovering a job by accident. Research shows that it is often *not* your immediate connections that will get you the next job, but rather **their connections**. Your five closest people in your network all have many connections. Your access to *their* networks comes through establishing good relationships and maintaining them with as many people as you can.

For example, when someone in my network comes to me about finding a new job, **I personally do not have a job for them**. What I hope is that **someone in my network can help this person**. It is the *extension* of my contacts that can really help people.

Let me get specific to help you understand the power of second connections, I currently have 1,530 LinkedIn 1st connections. This translates

to 2nd connections of more than 370,642! Your network can truly acceler-
ate your career. Each connection you make reflects an average of 400 new
people you can reach out to through that one connection. This translates
to hundreds of companies who may be looking for your skills and talents,
and an average of 500+ jobs. (Data from LinkedIn Official blog by Aatif
Awan).   https://blog.linkedin.com/2017/april/24/the-power-of-linkedins-
500-million-community

Outside Expert

My good friend Bob McIntosh, Job Search Strategist at MassHire
Lowell Career Center (we've never met face-to-face but I still consider him a friend through numerous online discussions and a number of zoom video-conference calls).

Shared with me his definition of networking: "Networking is
about connecting with people to form relationships that are beneficial to everyone *involved. It's also about expanding one's opportunities
by connecting with everyone they come into contact with.*"

**Again, networking is a two-way relationship that benefits
both people in some way.** If you coach your clients to think about
it as "relationship building," they might find it more palatable and
easier to take on.

Coaching in Action

One client I had recently was looking to work somewhere that
did "some type of good for society." We brainstormed organizations, agencies, and companies for her to explore. After talking
with a person in her network about this idea, her friend said she
could introduce my client to the CEO at Coastal Enterprises. In
her meeting with this CEO, she discovered another agency that
Coastal Enterprises works with that sounded interesting. She ended
up interviewing for a job at that company and was hired to be the
Executive Director. Her 1st connection (friend) introduced her to
the CEO (2nd connection), through which she discovered the 3rd
connection opportunity.

Help Your Clients Develop Their Networks—One Drop at a Time

Here are some major takeaways you should impart to your clients when you discuss the networking process.

Career development is all personal. People do not hire resumes. People do not connect with texts or emails. It's always been, and probably always will be, **human contact that matters.** Paper and electronic communication should only be the tools to create human contact or to maintain relationships.

Think of networking and "relationship building" as the drip on your faucet. You can fill a sink with a dripping faucet, but it will take a while. Relationship building does not happen by "turning on the faucet." The friends you have today did not happen because you walked up to a perfect stranger and hugged them! Oh my…that is a visual, isn't it? I can only imagine my hockey buddy Pete running away from me the first time we meet, and I hug him.

Your personal relationships took time to develop, and your professional ones will too. Here are some things your clients should think about as they consider professional relationship building. I recommend taking a few minutes each week and focus on one of these areas…drip…drop…drip…drop.

Connecting

No matter where you are in the process, start with one more connection. Don't send a blast to all 345 people in your address book—remember, it's one drip at a time. (And maybe friends won't appreciate being called a "drip," so don't tell them that.)

On LinkedIn, your clients should **think about people they worked for or with,** search them, go to their profile, and *connect.* Always change the standard LinkedIn request to something personal. Not too long but say why you are connecting.

Hi Jack, it's been awhile since I've seen you and I am interested in reconnecting here on LinkedIn. Hope all is well. Let me know if there is anything I can do for you.

Keep it simple and use your own voice—be real, be yourself.

If you are sending an email to someone like Jack above (not in LinkedIn, which limits characters) you may want to expand the email length a bit and give more details and make it more personal. Here's an example:

Hi Jack, it's been awhile since I've seen you. Since I saw you last we added another child to our household ... a little girl who it now 6 months old. I've decided to explore the possibility of a job change. A little more income would be great, but I'm looking for more challenge too. I still hope to work in the area of fabric manufacturing. While our two kids are still young, seems like a good opportunity to be open to relocating. Any leads or suggestions would sure be appreciated.

I hope that your family is well. Give my best to Cindy. Of course, if there is ever anything I can do for you, please let me know.

They key here is that you need to keep your network alive—one person, one email, one phone call, one coffee at a time.

When people connect on LinkedIn or Twitter (or wherever else you are)**, take a minute and send them a "thanks for connecting" reply.** If you can add any other relevant comments (*"How is that old Labrador retriever doing?"* or *"I look forward to learning more about what you do!"*), it will feel more like a relationship than a simple online/social media connection.

When you meet someone at a conference, workshop, or event, search for them and send a request to connect: *"So nice to have met you at the conference. I would like to connect here on LinkedIn, so we can continue to learn from each other."*

Ideas on How to Maintain Connections

Occasionally I will look through my contacts or groups I am involved with and reach out to ask if one of them would be willing to set up a video conference or phone call to discuss a project I am working on. Recently I asked two people to brainstorm some ideas with me using Skype. It was an awesome way to reconnect with two people I had not seen in a long time and to seek their advice. (Thanks Patrick and Beth!)

I have been inspired to continue sending out thank you cards by Jimmy Fallon, who sends thank you cards every Friday. I have a reminder that pops up on my calendar the third Saturday of every month to go through my contacts and think about who I can thank. I don't do it every third Saturday, but it reminds to pull out those thank you cards occasionally and express my gratitude.

Helping Clients Expand Their Network Via LinkedIn

Have your clients **look at the given LinkedIn suggestions** (Twitter does too) and scroll through the list. Often, I find people I "thought" I was connected with but am not. These are "warm connections" that are easy to add.

Clients can then look through their 1st connections and click on *their* "Connections" (Go to a 1st connection and simply click on their "connections" in the lower right of their picture). When browsing here, they may find people they already know, but more importantly, they may find people they **would like to connect with**.

At this point, you can:

- Ask your 1st connection to introduce you.
- Request to connect here. But remember, this is more of a "cold connect" because they don't know you; be sure and explain why you want to connect.
- Email them or call their office to set up an informational meeting seeking advice and getting to know them. (If you can find an email, it's always good to start with that—people tend to be pretty busy). After you meet with the person, you can ask to connect on LinkedIn.

Whether your client has started working on their professional relationships or not, stress that the process is a "drip…drop…drip…drop." Ask them to take a few minutes each week, or whenever they are **inspired**, to add a few people to their network or reach out and contact existing connections.

"It's Not What You Know…." cuts both ways

Sometimes knowing a person can be a problem. My mother-in-law has always stated, "It's not what you know, it's who you know." I argued with her once (only once) that you **have to know something *and* be a good person as well.** I *know* some people and I can guarantee I would *never* hire them!

As career coaches, we all know the power of networking and how important it is to find someone on the "inside" of a company—but that is only the first step. I know a college student who reached out to an alumnus with a clumsily written, grammatically incorrect email. That did not bode well for him (or the college). Other common missteps are typos on a resume/cover letter, or a lousy handshake, or even worse, bad breath. It can be stressful meeting someone who could be influential in your career but having less than 15 seconds in most cases to turn that into your advantage!

The message is that "networking works," but we need to make sure that people working with us don't think that just because "dad knows some-one at xyz company" they will be all set. They might be, but at the core we are instinctual people and we draw our own conclusions about peo-ple very quickly—sometimes in less than 2 seconds. A handshake takes less than 2 seconds (a 5-second handshake would be SO uncomfortable!), and a brief introductory email to an alumnus is read in less than 5 sec-onds. Sure, maybe a phone call could take a minute before an impression is made, but the major takeaway is that **impressions are made every time we contact people.**

So, what can we do to help our students/clients network better to make the best impressions?

1. Ask to review their **resume and cover letter** and tell them why we are doing it. (The answer? To make sure they make a great first impression). Most resumes are reviewed in less than 15 seconds, but even so, typos, grammar mistakes, formatting errors, etc, will be noticed.

2. Ask to review a **draft of correspondence** to be sent out to their net-work (on LinkedIn or via emails) and let them know an impression (good or bad) is made almost immediately upon opening it.

3. **Practice a handshake** and give them feedback. (This is particu-larly important for college students, and definitely true for interna-tional students) This high touch part of our culture can be a "make or break" for some, and it's all over in seconds.

4. Encourage **mock interviews**—not just for the content, but for the process as a whole. Consider the introductory time, walking into the reception area, small talk, and answering the most common first questions in the interview (which require a 1–2 minute answer that will set the tone for the rest of the interview).

5. Talk about **proper grooming** and habits such as chewing gum, turning off cell phones, dressing appropriately for informational and job interviews, etc. Not everyone needs each of these areas dis-cussed, but we can certainly emphasize the importance that presen-tation makes in those vital first 15 seconds.

Yes, 70-80% of all jobs are *not* advertised and yes, people have to develop a network and reach out, and yes, it helps to know someone, but instincts have kept us alive for thousands of years and **instincts will shut doors to job opportunities if your clients don't pay attention to them.** We need to remind our students/clients that there has to be substance as well, and first impressions via email, Twitter, Skype, Facebook, phone calls, and face-to-face meetings (heaven forbid a face to face meeting!) are so very important.

Relationship building is where your clients can learn.

As your clients learn the ins and outs of building a network via relationships, they will learn about how to do their jobs better. They will learn about other opportunities. They will learn who potential mentors are. Who you learn from is important and takes time. **We all learn daily, from infancy to old age.** We can't help it as our senses pull in information from a variety of sources. Then, we have to do something with that information.

A **great way for clients to learn is to identify people they can model.** Have them think about an area where they need more information, like using social media to research their industry, or new ideas on developing a project at work, improving their mental health, how to advance in their careers—whatever you need help on right now. Now have clients go to their LinkedIn contacts page, business cards, cell phone contacts, email contacts (any place they have lists of contacts) and look for people who can help them. Devise a plan to reach out to them and ask if they could help figure out the issue at hand, learn more about it, or guide them to resources that could help. **Call these people what you want (a network, resources, or mentors), but we all have them and we should all *be* one for others.**

It has been said that we are the average of our six closest friends. I believe we are also the average of our six closest people in your professional network. In my life, Rees models calm and thoughtful communication. Barry is my inspiration to read. Sabrina reminds me about mindfulness. Mark the importance of relationships.

Think about your role models. Do you need another one to help in an area? Do you need to thank one of them for their inspiration? Have your clients do the same.

Here are 4 tips on how your clients can find people to model.

1. **Identify people in their company** who have areas of knowledge they want. Then watch what they do and ask them questions.

2. **Identify people who have been in their company or industry for 20 years or more.** Watch what they do and ask them questions about their *perspective* on situations. This historical knowledge may not have all the "bells and whistles" of the newest way of doing things but can be rich in perspective.

3. **Think about your areas of weakness in their work.** Who out there, in their company or in industry, can they identify as a role model? They might find them on LinkedIn groups, presenting at conferences, leading in-service trainings, or in professional journals. Reach out to them and ask for advice.

4. **Look around at younger people or new people in their company.** What do they have that might be helpful to them? Is there a way for them to reach out to them and offer assistance? Of course, they should not come across like they have all the answers but lend a hand as a way of supporting their professional development.

We live in an "open source" world where by helping others, you can often help yourself in the long run.

- Learn from doing.
- Learn from watching.
- Learn from asking for help or information.
- Learn from actually helping others
- But whatever you do ... learn.

Networking, connections, relationship building ... regardless of what you decide to call it, the power of these relationship to move a client's career development forward cannot be overstated.

Career Coach Tips

- With most job positions not advertised (upwards of 80% are not) your network is most likely how people will find their next job. This is true for you and your clients.
- Think of networking as "relationship building"—a mutually beneficial relationship that involves learning from others and helping others.
- Networking takes time, just like any other relationship you have. Take the longer view and begin developing professional relationships one person at a time.

CHAPTER 6

Honoring All Career Pathways

"Community colleges play an important role in helping people transition between careers by providing the retooling they need to take on a new career."

—Barack Obama

"A high school diploma will no longer be sufficient. But that post-secondary education does not have to be a four-year university or four-year college. It can be career technical education, vocational education, community college."

—Raja Krishnamoorthi, American businessman, public servant, and politician from the state of Illinois who is the U.S. Representative for Illinois's 8th congressional district (2016–present)

We live in a world with a complex economy that's constantly in flux, where technology drives so many changes and creates new jobs at an amazing rate. As a result, many companies seek people with the skills needed these new jobs. The idea that "college for all" could solve the needs of our economy today is simply rubbish. Companies need more agility, and shorter-term training opportunities lead to a more agile workforce. Don't get me wrong, we will always need people with a bachelor's degree or more. But only about 30% of all jobs in our economy require this type of advanced degree.

The Georgetown University Center on Education and the Workforce defines "good paying jobs" as those that pay more than $35,000 a year for people ages 25-44. The middle-skills pathway is comprised of workers with more education than a high school diploma, but less than a bachelors, including certificates, certifications, licenses, associate degrees, and some college coursework. This pathway is in the midst of major transformation from traditional blue-collar jobs to more skilled technical jobs across skilled-services and blue-collar industries. In contrast to high school jobs, this pathway continues to grow. Workers with middle skills have 16 million good jobs, or 24% of all good jobs. (Three Educational Pathways To Good Jobs report http://bit.ly/peakcareers110)

We must remember that each of our clients is unique and brings an individual perspective of the world. Our job is to help them navigate their career development through our coaching, resources, and knowledge. You also must remember that each of us brings our own perspective of the world and that we all have "blind spots." We cannot possibly know all the occupations and career pathways available.

As a school counselor for 10 years my view of career development was shaped by the fact that in high school was on a college prep track, I attended a four-year college, went on for master's degree, and then worked in K-12 settings. You can see how it would be easy to say, "This worked for me, I think others should do this." But… (there's always a but) all segments of our economy need bright problem solvers who have good communication skills. Why would bachelor's degree majors be the only route? Don't you want your plumber or electrician or mechanic to have those same skills?

Challenge yourself to fight the "college for all" mentality. It simply is more complex than that. The economy is surely more complex, as less than 30% of all jobs require a four-year college degree.

Our job as career coaches and practitioners is to help our students and clients discover a career by exploring pathways that match their strengths and interests. Then, we help them get onto and navigate these pathways, whether it is via apprenticeship, bachelor's degree, trade school, or certificate. All too often, I hear people say they will go to college and figure it out there. That is a very expensive and time-consuming method of career exploration. I do get the sense that the "college for all" mentality is slowing down, but we still have a long way to go.

The message that everyone should go to college to be successful has hurt our economy a couple different ways:

1. Many people attended college who should not have been there and incurred lots of debt they have to pay back.
2. Some of those people only left with debt and some college credits—and no degree.

3. Those same people could have been working during that time and making money.

4. Many of those people would have been happier in trades and technical positions, which are in need of people.

One problem, in my opinion, is that we have too many colleges in our country fighting over the same high school graduates. A college's motivation is to fill seats, not to help these people discover their best career pathways. We have started to see higher education institutions closing down, and I think we will see more (and should see) more close in the future.

I was thrilled that President Obama chose to highlight two-year colleges in his eight years in office. Finally, we were placing emphasis on alternate career pathways to success besides four-year colleges. Community colleges play a vital role in training people for a variety of trade, technical, and health professions in short-term educational career pathways. And if they want, students can do both—earn 60 credits at a community college, save money, explore, and then transfer to a bachelor's degree.

Offering the option of exploring career pathways needs to start much earlier in schools, and we need to ensure that we are honoring all jobs. Another issue is that school counselors are dealing with so many issues in schools these days that career planning often takes a backseat. Even the job title has changed from "guidance counselor," one who provides guidance, to "school counselor," which is much more multi-faceted. Having been a school counselor for a decade, I know all too well the pressures they face.

On his website, Bryan Alexander says that "Goldman Sachs shared their analysis of higher education for investors a few weeks ago, and it's an important document for people in higher education to consider. Goldman is enormously influential in the finance world, and also in government, two realms with a lot of clout in academic institutions. **Is the ROI of attending college worth it?**" Read his analysis here http://bit.ly/peakcareers111

"Marc Miller of Career Pivot stated that in Houston the group of people with a degree who has the highest unemployment rate are those with law degrees, with 18% unemployment" and Taylor Pearson says "we may have crossed the threshold of whether a Master's degree is worth it as an investment. with the exception of some hard sciences."

CGI, a local software company in Waterville, ME, is hiring like crazy right now and they do not care if you have a degree or not. They are looking for people who are curious and like to solve problems—young people who are creating apps for phones, for example, are great potential employees.

I'd like to also point out that the Brookings Institute in 2013 stated that half of all STEM jobs did NOT require a four-year degree. IBM calls these "new collar jobs" (no degree required). So, when we think of science skills/aptitudes we need to remember that many jobs require these skills, from technicians to scientists.

Career pathways are like trailheads.
They all lead to someplace great.

Regardless of the pressure to serve so many counseling needs in the schools, we *must* do more in our schools to introduce students to different career choices and to make sure we are respecting all career pathways, including trade, technical, and construction positions, and others. These discussions should include the possibility of apprenticeships, short-term training certificates, and associate degrees, as well as the more common bachelor's degree options.

I recently attended a Chamber of Commerce meeting where we had a large construction firm,

Sheridan Corporation, talk about their needs. There is such a shortage of workers in the construction field. But what amazing opportunities exist there! The industry struggles with the stigma that all construction jobs are dirty, there is a lot of travel to job sites, and that it is a dead-end job. Sure, when starting out in the construction field the first two can often be correct, but the dead-end job stigma is very far from the truth.

Sheridan Corporation offers on-the-job training and mentorships, pays for training and education, provides transportable credentials, encourages their employees to look for internal opportunities, and trains their supervisors to give frequent feedback and encouragement to their employees. There will always be a need for entry-level construction/tradespeople, and now there are more opportunities than ever to grow in a company.

With technology integrated into all aspects of the construction industry, there will always be a need for more short-term training. Companies will need someone to pound the nail, but they may also be asking that person to use GPS to determine *where the building is laid out*. They also need the foreman to know how to navigate a complete set of plans available on an iPad on site, and heavy equipment that tells the operator, "This is too heavy to lift." The opportunities are many.

We need all jobs to be honored in this country. It is clear this is not often the case.

There are tens of thousands of jobs that do not require a college degree that are wonderful choices for people—and *yes*, pay very good money. I know many people who have great jobs with no bachelor's degree, from a great career in the radio business, to jobs in auto mechanics, HVAC, and many others. Businesses in the trades/crafts areas are desperate for bright people who can problem solve and produce quality work. Why do we shuffle *every* student who is bright in math/science to college? If they want to work with their hands and produce goods, why wouldn't we make it okay for them to choose a trade? I think of the German model of education that provides two different tracks in high school, allowing bright young men and women who want to work in a craft or trades area to get the training they need... and it is okay to do this, not a lesser option like it is here.

My personal biases changed when **I serendipitously ended up at a high school vocational center and it *changed my life*!** I saw very intelligent students doing amazing craft work who often struggled to pass their high school classes. It taught me a lesson I have never forgotten.

The fact that many of my uncles worked in the construction field helped me to see a different side of our society, but it wasn't until I worked at the technical center that I finally understood. My uncles were masons, carpenters, electricians, and train engineers and suddenly I "got it." Here

If you have not read Shop Class As Soul Craft by Matthew Crawford, you should. (Read my book review here http://bit.ly/peakcareers112). He has a PhD in Philosophy and was working for a professional journal writing abstracts but was always drawn back to his work on motorcycles and the problem-solving skills it took to do that job. Matthew is one of many people who probably was given one choice in high school: "You are bright, you are going to college."

Matthew argues that our country has failed an entire population of people by continuing to cut shop classes high school technical education for those people that can't go to college. (Notice I said, "can't go to college," which is loaded with all kinds of implications. Because they do not *look* like they are college material? They don't learn best by reading? Because they are poor? This list goes on and on.)

are highly skilled, intelligent, problem solvers that made a very good living. They all chose differently than me but made good choices nonetheless. Don't you want the plumbers, mechanics, or electricians you hire to be great problem solvers with the intelligence to fix your problem? Then we need to encourage bright boys and girls to consider these options. And guess what? You cannot send this type of skilled labor overseas to get done—this type of problem solving must stay here.

We as career practitioners need to pay attention to our biases. To view the world of work in its totality. To give another storyline to all professions, and to honor all jobs in this country. Teachers, school counselors, principals, college faculty, parents, and other leaders need to make it okay for young people to choose something besides going to a four-year college.

Our great country cannot afford to ignore the many wonderful craft/trade options available: our economy needs it, our communities need it, and most importantly, individuals with these talents need to know it is okay to work in the trades.

Please be clear, **I am huge supporter of *all* types of education** and believe strongly in the liberal arts education, graduate work, bachelor's, and associate degrees. But we must recognize, support, and give honor to all career pathways—not just higher education.

Career Coach Tips

- Focus on your client or student's strengths, values, passions, and interests, and listen to what they are really communicating (not just what they are saying).
- Honor all jobs and all career pathways. Be aware we all have biases.
- Check and confront your biases and your client's/student's biases.
- Have your clients and students explore all career pathways, including apprenticeships, on-the-job training, certificates/diplomas, and every other option for our clients and students. There are many ways to get to an end.
- My last challenge is to do what you can to affect real change in our communities by honoring and respecting all career pathways.

CHAPTER 7

It's All About the Conversation

"Through my experience and research, I've identified five key strategies that help facilitate a productive dialogue. They are: be curious, check your bias, show respect, stay the course, and end well."

—Celeste Headlee, Author of We Need to Talk:
How to Have Conversations that Matter

"Good listeners have a huge advantage. For one, when they engage in conversation, they make people 'feel' heard. They 'feel' that someone really understands their wants, needs and desires. And for good reason; a good listener does care to understand.

—Simon Sinek British-American author,
motivational speaker and organizational consultant."

As career coaches, we must always remember that **it is all about the conversation**. It is not about the assessments we give, or the advice we hand out, or even the resources we share. Without a quality conversation we cannot be that helpful to our clients. By discussing assessment results and consistently checking in with our clients, they can then learn how to interpret whether they are on the right track.

When I was the Director of Advising, Career, and Transfer at a local community college, I taught a Career Decision Making class. I gave three different interest assessments, one personality (MBTI), and two values assessments. As a I prepared the students for each one I would say, "Don't believe the results of the assessments". They'd look at me confused and typically ask, "Then why are we taking them?" I'd explained they should be suspicious of all assessment results. It isn't until we discuss the results and make sense of them within each person's specific life and situation that we can believe them.

In sum, **assessments are just sophisticated prompts**. They are tools designed to stimulate the conversation.

At a high school technical center where I worked for six years, we had an assessment lab that measured skills, interests, and aptitudes. There were times I would meet with students to discuss their results and would literally rip them up and throw them out because they were not helpful or informative. Students wanted so badly to be told what program or occupation to go into, but the results gave a list of occupations that were simply not what they were remotely interested in and were primarily entry level jobs that required no training.

Be critical of all assessments you use. There is no need to keep results that make a student feel disappointed, or worse, try to *make* one of the occupations work for them. It's best to change the conversation to what to do next—not focus on an assessment that gives bad information.

The purpose of doing assessments is to help the client understand themselves better in the context of career development. You may determine your client needs help clarifying their interests, or values, or personality better. You then choose the best assessment that measures what you are trying to measure. But we should not be doing the same assessment to every client "just to do an assessment". Make sure you are using the right tool for the job.

Assessments give your client another way to understand themselves and to look at the situation from another perspective. I can still remember when I took the Myers-Briggs assessment years ago and realized that not everyone saw the world as I did! It is one thing to take an assessment and get the results. It is another thing to understand those results and to put it in context. It is all about the conversation.

The Magic of Card Sorts

The longer I have been doing career coaching, the fewer formal assessments I use. I used to administer the Strong Interest Inventory and the Myers-Briggs Type Indicator quite often with students. These are great assessments that give useful information. They only give information and without a conversation, the client does not always internalize the information to help them move forward in their career development.

I now use card sorts much more often. Although there many different card sorts, I especially like **skills card sorts**. If a client can already identify the skills they have that they want to continue to use, there is no need. But many clients have a difficult time articulating their skills, and card sorts are great informal assessments to help people through that process.

So why do most people like card sorts? Each time they hold a skill card in their hand they are processing how the skill fits into their lives. Informal assessments like card sorts do not give a list of jobs to consider. They don't *give* the client anything—the *client* is the one that does everything. Clients place the cards in a category or a gradient (such as Like Using /Don't Like or Proficient/Need More Training) and decide which cards to keep or remove. They own the process. I've had students do the skills card sorts, look at their skills on the table, and become so ecstatic to **see themselves right there on the table**. I had one senior at Colby College say, "Who wouldn't want to do this? These are all the skills I love using."

I typically have clients do three sorts. Each time, they roll the given word around in their heads, thinking about how they use the skill, where they use it, if they like it a lot or a little, and anything else that comes to mind. When we get to the final sort, the skills on the table are truly representative of the person—there is seldom a lack of words to describe them.

I often use **Knowdell's Motivated Skills Card Sorts** when exploring skills with a client. I also use **SkillScan** cards. Knowdell first has clients sort

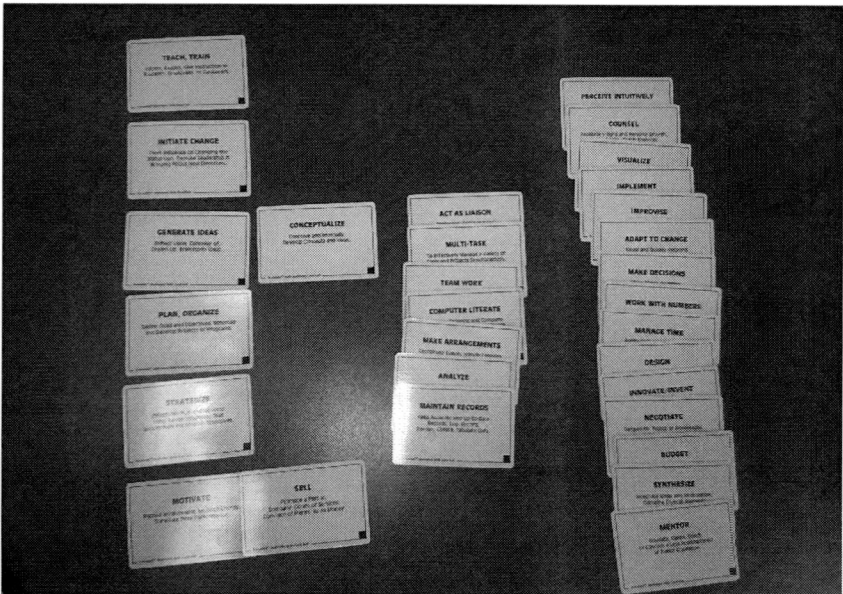

by which skills they like to use, from "Totally Delight in Using" down to "Strongly Dislike Using." Then he directs the client to take those piles and sort them by how skilled they are, from "Highly Proficient" to "Competent" to "Lack Desired Skill." This gives a matrix of cards with the "motivated skills" in the upper left corner. (Delight using and highly proficient). This is where Knowdell stops. I then have the clients take all the cards in their "Totally Delight" and "Enjoy Using Very Much" rows and I say, "Sort these into groups or themes that make sense to you."

Because of what I call the "Magic of Card Sorts," by this point clients have thought about each skill at least three times, so they rarely have trouble moving the 12-20 cards into groups or themes that make sense to them. When they are done, I say, "Tell me about your groups or themes." This is where the conversation begins and the connections are made with the clients. I ask, "Which groups are **must haves**" in your next job? Which groups could you live without?"

This conversation helps clients articulate what is important to them and how certain skills fit into their career development. Often, for the first time, they are able to identify specific skills they want to use in future jobs. We use this to develop their value-added statement.

The Value-Added Statement

Here is how I work with clients to create this statement. Using the skills card sort to identify skills they want and enjoy using, they then identify groups or themes they see with those skills and how they fit into their career development. They then create a bulleted list of the 5 or 6 essential skills and interests they bring to an employer. Often this is revealed in the groups or themes they worked on, but it certainly comes out of the conversation and questions I ask them when processing the card sort. I take notes during our conversation about the cards on the table and I am looking for *their words and phrases* they use.

Some clients will also complete a values card sort to help them understand how values fit into their decisions. When people talk about the importance of company "fit" it often has to do with values.

After they create their bulleted list of the 5 or 6 essential things they want everyone to know about them (sort of like an elevator pitch, but I like the focus to be on "value-added" rather than a pitch), they then work on a summary statement.

Here are two sample value-added statements.

A Senior Multimedia Professional with 10 years of experience in video production, marketing, and corporate communications. Exceeding expectations for clients in corporate, educational, industrial, and legal settings is my mission. Effective, compelling, and modern storytelling through words and images is the means. Looking for opportunities to become a valued contributor with a mid-sized or larger organization in the Greater Portland, ME, region."

Note: The one below includes a 'tag line' that can also be discovered through this process. Often it comes out when they are telling stories to support their "5 or 6 essentials things they want everyone to know about them."

Catalyst for Positive Change – Saving one life at a time changes many lives

As a visionary, passionate, and mission-driven leader, I have a well-established reputation for bringing out the best in peopl and teams, building client-centered communications strategies and systems, and creating inclusive relationships based on trust and mutual respect.

A professional communications professional with more than 20 years of experience, I thrive in a creative, thoughtful work environment that is collaborative, engaged and dedicated to the welfare of people suffering from behavioral health issues, and respectful of their journeys.

These value-added statements are then used to create Professional Summaries at the top of a resume, a LinkedIn Summary section, cover letters, and the message they will say to everyone they know.

Talk Less, Nudge More

According to brain-based research (the Brain-Based Career Development Theory by Imants Jaunarajs, Jodi Pavol, and Erin Morgenstern), the goal of the career coach is to talk about 20% of the time. We should help the client think through the process and come to their own conclusions. We, of course, are there to nudge and ask questions that help them reveal answers—answers that make sense to them, not just answers that we hand them.

I was a school counselor and a career counselor for years. At first, I was reluctant to use the term "career coach" because there were so many people out there working as coaches with little training. I was also an academic advisor. Counselors and advisors, by definition, counsel and give advice. But that is not what I wanted to do when working with clients. I wanted to help people make their own decisions. I now call myself a "career coach" because this terminology establishes a more supportive relationship.

Granted, I still have the word "counselor" on my website in a few places because that is what people search for, but the emphasis on the website and in my practice is now on coaching.

I still provide counsel, advice, and resources. But by calling myself a "coach" it changes the relationship a bit and reminds me to stay focused on the client talking more and me less.

We need to listen carefully to where each person is today in their career development and take each person at their face value. Aim to listen *first*, to understand a client's specific situation and then proceed in a way that benefits that individual. I think there were a few years where I gave too many students similar assessments and the same resources and did not take the time to slow down and really listen to what each person was saying to me.

I think about my two oldest sons, Chris and Cody, and how their basketball coach dealt with them. The coach was a yeller—not abusive, but still a yeller. He called the kids out during the games and practices. Chris could take it and was even motivated by it. Cody ...not so much. I actually went to talk to the coach because I worked in the same school as he did, and I knew him well. I suggested to him that Cody was different than Chris. Cody responded much better when you took him out of the spotlight and explained what you wanted him to do differently in a more private setting.

That is a good lesson for all of us career coaches. Each person is different, even though they may look the same. It's easy when you are seeing hundreds of students and they all "look the same" to give them the same assignments and resources. But each person is an individual and at a different stage of their career development.

Focus on the Client

"What would you like to accomplish today?" This can be a great start to your client session, even if you have given homework and already decided what you wanted to cover. I've had clients who had worked on one assignment like the value-added statement, where our goal was to practice it and then work on the LinkedIn profile that day, only to ask **what they would like to work on today** and discovered there is a job they wanted to apply for that they discovered the day before. That was what they wanted to talk about.

Think about that. If you were in the client's seat and all you could think about was how to apply to a job, and the career coach was rambling on about LinkedIn just because that was the plan, you would not be paying attention. Your mind would be running, thinking about everything but LinkedIn. Ask the client every session what they want to work on first. If they choose something themselves, they are more likely to listen, invest themselves in the process, and actually learn something.

Too often career coaches are so busy and want to give each person the same information and resources **because we know they work**. The trouble is, if the client isn't listening or processing the information, it doesn't matter if it is good or if worked with 100 other students. Focus on the client and make sure you are helping them with what they need that day and that time.

Open Ended Questions

- Here is a sampling of questions you could use to get your clients/students talking and thinking.
- What would you like to accomplish or work on today?
- What have you done so far to find work or explore options?
- What energizes you?
- What information is missing for you that you need in order to make a decision?
- What are the two most important things in your life today?
- What themes do you see in your life? (i.e., Did you always look to help people or train people? Did you always present at conferences, and why?)
- What are your top skills, strengths, passions, interests, and values? (This should be broken into multiple questions—don't overwhelm them.)
- Ask someone who is undecided about their career to describe their "job from hell." After they've listed several things (which isn't hard!) ask them to do a 180 and tell what the opposite of each item could look like. That more positive list is a good place to look. (This bullet idea is from Dan Kennedy, Professional Personal and Executive Coach)
- How did you choose your major or past occupation(s)?
- What makes you unique in the workplace? What are your top 3-5 skills, strengths, and talents at work?

(Continued on next page)

(Continued from previous page)

- What do you want to be most known for at work?
- What engages you? What are you excited or passionate about? (Think about the times you have been in "flow" at work and lost track of time.)
- How would some of your co-workers describe your strengths? (and/or friends and family)
- What type of work, or tasks at work, provide you the most joy and sense of fulfillment?
- What do you see as the patterns of your life? Themes that keep coming back?
- If you could change five things in the world or community, what would it be?
- What are the top two or three most important things in your life today? Why?
- What have always been your most natural abilities—the courses you "aced" in school, the skills that always came easily to you?
- Name something positive and something negative people have told you all your life about yourself.
- What would you say is the most satisfying accomplishment of your life so far?
- What are you passionately curious about and fascinated by? What do you love to study and research, write about, blog about, investigate, and try to understand?
- What is your favorite quality about yourself?
- What does "networking" mean to you?
- What are some things you could do now to increase your network?
- How are you currently using LinkedIn?
- Are there people on LinkedIn you would like to connect with? What are some strategies you could do to connect and find people?

In the fall of 2018, I attended a Maine Career Development Association workshop on Brain-Based Career Development Theory that supported so much of my thinking with research. When this synergy happens, it just gives me more confidence to continue working. It also helps me refine some of my work.

Here are my six big takeaways.

1. The brain can only handle four pieces of information in the prefrontal cortex; two is best. This means we need to work hard to focus on one major task at a time. Most of us have many more thoughts going on at once.

2. Remember our students/clients are coming with lots of things on their mind and we need to help them focus. Don't overload them with lots of tasks. Narrow the issues down to three or four and then focus on one at a time, even if it means more meetings.

3. Keep the focus on the student/client: "What would you like to accomplish today?"

4. Set clear expectations for the time you have with them. (Again, don't overload them; describe your role in the process and check in with them about halfway through the session to make sure they are understanding it.)

5. Help them find their solutions with your coaching. The goal is for you to talk 20% of time.

6. Assign action steps that can be accomplished in 2-5 days.

Coaching in Action

I felt good about my practice after attending the Brain-Based Career Development Theory workshop and after reading the monograph, but realized with one client, in particular, I had overloaded him. He had recently dropped out of college about halfway through his first semester, and his dad wanted him to have some career coaching. I assigned lots of homework because I figured he had all kinds of time on his hands and wanted to get moving. I failed miserably. I now know I must have overwhelmed him. I really should have shortened up our meetings, broken the assignments into smaller bits, and checked in with him more often. Lessened learned.

Career Coach Tips

- Keep the focus on the client. What do they need and want during the session?
- If you do use assessments, make sure the focus is on the conversation around the results and what the information means to them.
- Try to keep the client talking for the majority of the session by asking open-ended, thought-provoking questions. This helps clients figure it out on their own and will lead them to produce action steps they are committed to.
- Assign homework that is doable in the client's timeframe that can give them insight and make them feel like they are progressing. Through this, you can determine their level of commitment.

CHAPTER 8

Self-Care for the Career Coach: Being a better you is better for your clients

"Mindfulness is deliberately paying full attention to what is happening around you and within you—in your body, heart, and mind. Mindfulness is awareness without criticism or judgment."

—Jan Chozen Bays, Author of *How to Train a Wild Elephant: And Other Adventures in Mindfulness*

In our ever-busy world, it is important we find ways to slow ourselves down to better serve ourselves and clients. Our ability to manage the tsunami of information coming into us daily (even hourly!) is inversely linked to the quality of services we provide. If we are constantly chasing emails, tweets, and other social media messages, we are not taking the time to slow down and "think." Yes, just "think"—instead of reacting. (Read my blog titled A Nation on Speed here http://bit.ly/peakcareers113)

Mindfulness can be as simple as taking three deep breaths and focusing on the breathing. It can be downloading an App like Calm, closing your eyes and listening to the sound of the ocean for two minutes. You could go for a walk and <u>not</u> listen to a podcast or music and just walk focusing on the muscles you are using, the sound around you, and clearing your mind of the 100's of ideas and things to do. Calming down our 'monkey brain' which wants to leap from place to place is the goal.

Here are some reasons why you should practice mindfulness as a career practitioner.

1. It leads to creativity

In the May 2017 issue of *National Geographic*, there was an article about what made geniuses different than other people.

"...the aha moment, the flash of clarity that arises at unexpected times—in a dream, in the shower, on a walk—often emerges after a period of contemplation. Information comes in consciously, but the problem is processed unconsciously, the resulting solution leaping out when the mind least expects it."

Sigmund Freud walked every day after his mid-day meal. He knew that reflective time was an important routine to help him think. Daily reflection is important because it dedicates time and space for you to solve problems. **Giving yourself time to *reflect* daily is a sign of self-respect.** It honors your true self (not the hurried one) and gives you permission to be creative by finding time in your busy day. We do work that changes daily with the clients we serve, and the ability to find creative solutions to problems is a great way to better serve them.

There is a reason people say they got their idea when taking a shower. You are alone, no distractions, and your mind is typically not jumping around. Slowing your mind down is often where creativity is born.

2. Energy

I started doing Qi Gong, which is like Tai Chi. It is a physical way to slow down each day and focus my thoughts on physical movements in a purposeful way. I have found there are a number of Qi Gong movements that bring more energy to my day, and they are very simple to do at any time throughout the day.

Going for a walk outdoors or sitting at a park bench being 'present' in the moment can have many benefits. There is quite a bit of research out there that shows people get energy from being outdoors near trees. I read one study that said even looking at pictures of nature can cause mental energy to bounce back. (Business Insider April 22, 2016)

This does not have to be a lot of time, but how about making it a "thoughtful" time. What I mean by that is you must be intentional about finding this time daily and take those few minutes to take a walk on your break, walk with a client for 10 minutes to start a meeting, or download the Google Chrome extension Momentum that has a beautiful outdoor picture and inspirational quote every time you open a new tab.

3. It leads to higher quality work

I was working with a client recently who said she used to respond to every email as quickly as she could at any time of the day or night. Her customers then expected her to get back to her at all hours of the day or weekends. She finally realized she was not doing quality work that she was proud of.

So, she changed to reading her emails periodically throughout the day (I do this too). She will often read an email, think about how to respond, and then set it aside and come back to it in an hour or so.

She said, "The quality of my work improves when I do this, my composition of my email is better, and I feel like I am respecting myself more *and* respecting my client's needs." It does not take long for the clients to realize they *will* get an answer and it will be a good answer; it just may not happen immediately.

> ## From the American Mindfulness Research Association. 6/13/2018
>
> **Bostock et al. (*Journal of Occupational Health Psychology*)** conducted a randomized, controlled study of whether a mindfulness app, as a lower-cost alternative to in-person training, could reduce work-related stress among corporate employees.
>
> The mindfulness group showed significantly greater improvement on wellbeing (partial $\eta2=.04$), mood ($\eta2=.04$), depression ($\eta2=.03$), anxiety ($\eta2=.005$), job strain ($\eta2=.04$), and perceived workplace social support ($\eta2=.07$). Further analysis of job strain showed that perceived job control improved even though perceived job demands remained the same.

It seems counter intuitive that slowing down can actually improve your work day, but our brains need a break from the busyness. It is one reason we need sleep and that we dream. Daniel Pink in his latest book, *When: The Scientific Secrets of Perfect Timing* talks about even taking a 25 minute nap around 2:30pm as a way to reboot your energy for the remainder of the day. (Read my book review of When here http://bit.ly/peakcareers114)

Regardless of what you do, find a way to slow down each day and you will see the results in your work.

The Importance of Establishing Routines

Whatever you do to increase your mindfulness, make it a routine. Like a muscle, your brain can grow with practice. If you make moments of self care a routine in your day, your ability to be more mindful will greatly improve.

I take 20 minutes most every morning to do Qi Gong before breakfast; I then take a few minutes before or after breakfast to journal and capture my thoughts for the day. I try to take a short walk right after lunch every day. Then, at 2:30 I have an "appointment" that is in my calendar to take a mindfulness break. The key is to find time daily to "be" in the moment and to *be quiet*. From this quiet time will come the creativity you are often looking for, the energy to work, and that sense of calm that often brings quality work.

Want to take this to another level? In Richard Leider's book *Repacking Your Bags* he talks about the importance of taking a full day off with no electronics—a sort of sabbatical from the internet, phones, and all communication. My brother Mark has been doing this for years. He has inspired me to make this a priority. I now look for one day each month to take my "social media/electronic retreat". There are months I simply can't do it, but I rarely miss two in a row. (Read my book review of RePacking Your Bags here http://bit.ly/peakcareers115)

One of my Peak-Careers Advisory Board members, after reading my first business plan (which was very ambitious) asked me, "When are you going to find time to just stop and think?" I realized there were lots of great ideas but little time to slow down and reflect. I've never forgotten his question.

What my brother Mark does is take his retreats on the months that have five Fridays, which gives him four retreats each year. Because it is the fifth Friday, there are never any standing meetings, and it feels like an extra day in the month. I have more flexibility, so I look at my months and determine a day (typically a Friday) that I won't be too crunched the following week, and then arrange to go somewhere. These retreats cannot be done at your home. I now do them in an office space available to me. I have at times gone to the local public library (built in the late 1800s with Carnegie money, it has some great sitting rooms), and have even found a room at Colby College here in town that gives me a quiet space with a view out of the chapel.

The first time I did this was crazy hard. I kept wanting to look at my cell phone and check emails and text messages, but I kept it off. I journaled about my time that morning and my business in general. I read a couple of journal articles I had been wanting to read, I meditated, and I just took time to think.

How often do you just take the time to think about things? That was the best advice my Advisory Board member could have given me at that time. I always feel like I need to *do* more, cram more things on my "to do" list. Accomplish more, more, more. But the time I've set aside to think has resulted in so much creativity and has kept me focused on what is important.

I have always made my retreats as close to eight-hours as possible, but you can start with a four-hour retreat. One person who was taking my Facilitating Career Development (FCD) class tried a four-hour retreat to start. She found it difficult but rewarding and hopes to do a full-day retreat sometime in the future. The important thing is to train the brain to slow down – turn off that 'monkey brain' once in a while.

These retreats are the days that I do "big" thinking. What do I want to happen over the next three months? What are the career topics I want to write about and share with my Peak-Careers community? Who would I like to interview? (I do monthly interviews of people on career topics). Do I have a topic to share on Facebook Live? What can I expect to happen with my business over the next 3, 6,12 months?

When I have finished my eight hours, I always feel so relaxed and inspired. I'm relaxed because many of the small things on my mind have been boxed up and taken care of. I focused on the big things. When you do this, you realize that some of those small things can actually be let go. I'm inspired because now instead of seeing only my "to do" list with 50 things on it in front of me, I can now see the long view of my work and it reminds of *why I do what I do.*

The longer the retreat, the better. In 2016 I was on a 100-mile backpack trip with my kindred spirit, my backpacking buddy Rees. It was nine days on the Pacific Crest Trail in southern California on the edge of the Mojave Desert. Not everyone can take such a trip, but I have to say there is nothing like this quality time of walking 12-15 miles on a trail with another person to talk about our lives, with no interruptions from technology. One day we took the afternoon to do "walking meditation". (Learn more at https://www.wildmind.org/walking/introduction)

This was a wonderful afternoon for both of us as we cleared our minds. What always amazes me is the creativity that comes after a day like this! **I get some of my best ideas to problems when I *stop thinking!***

Mindfulness to Better Serve Your Clients

We can help our clients in their career development by being more fully present in the moment. By appreciating the value of turning off technology and taking time to "think" prepares us to serve our clients better. By embracing these mindfulness basics, we help our clients by being more fully 'present' and often will come up with ideas or solutions to problems they face by being healthier ourselves. You don't have to spend hours meditating to be totally in the moment. Often the path to mindfulness is brief, simple, and even unexpected.

My wife asked for an adult coloring book for Christmas one year. I had no idea what that was, but she has one now ... and she loves it! Why? It has to do with mindfulness. Being present in the moment. No technology. Working on something tactile. She has to focus, which clears her mind. It can be challenging—but rewarding.

When I was enrolled in a three-week online class with Richard Leider called "Discover What's Next: Living Your Life on Purpose," affiliated with Life Reimagined, **one thing t**hat struck me was the power of journaling. I simply wrote my thoughts on what is important to me and obstacles I was facing. More importantly what I learned was that taking the time to process my thinking forced me to slow down. The simple act of writing with a writing instrument on paper made me think through my thoughts and clarified them in the process. It's not coloring books, but clearly a slowing-down process.

By journaling my thoughts, Richard Leider was forcing me to clarify and simplify things in my life. When thoughts are left in our heads they can feel "complicated" and confusing. Leider encourages journaling to take those thoughts in our heads and to get them onto paper where you can really see what they are and what they mean. This process is one step in discovering your purpose.

- When weaving mindfulness into your own professional and personal life, ask yourself:
- Can your clients find clarity in their career development and get closer to discovering their purpose through journaling?
- Can you be a better coach/counselor by taking a few moments daily to write down key thoughts?

The lesson for me is that we need *time* and *space* to think about our situations in order to process clearly, and so do your clients.

- Should your clients take a "time and space" break from job searching if they feel burnt out? If so, how can you help them structure this time?
- So many people feel overwhelmed in their daily expectations. How can you build in a break from "plowing through" your own daily work? You really do not have to make a huge time commitment to feel better.
- Do you have clients who come in and are stressed out? Could you have them try one of these stress relievers so your session will be more productive?
- Are you running from emails, to appointments, to meetings? Could you be a better coach/counselor if you took three deep breaths in between appointments and made sure you are totally focused on the task or person at hand?
- What if you met with a client in a "walking meeting" and you took the first five minutes to try "walking meditation?"

Not everyone will want to color or backpack 100 miles, but I believe both clients and counselors/coaches can benefit from integrating some of the lessons of mindfulness into our busy lives. Take time to calm yourself, breathe, reflect, and make sure you are totally and completely present. I believe you will be a better counselor/coach because of it.

So where to start?

Keep it simple. When our kids were young, we asked them every night before they went to bed, "Did you have anything sad happen today?" And then we asked for their final thought of the day, "What was your happy thought today?" They ended each day thinking about something happy. **Why don't you start with just slowing down and thinking about what makes you happy?**

Make a pledge to yourself to slow down for a bit every day. Find a time each day that works for you—maybe it is the morning like Mark, or midday like me, or at the end of the day. Simply reflect, think, unwind, leave the world of technology, and calm yourself. Find a quiet time for even 10 minutes to *think*, with no purpose other than to S-L-O-W-D-O-W-N. Find some peace...think positive thoughts...remove the clutter. Ten minutes.

Career Coach Tips

- By taking care of ourselves we are able to better serve our clients.
- Slowing down and being more mindful of the moment is often where you'll find creativity and solutions to problems.
- Creating routines in your life is how you enact change.
- When you have a client who appears frazzled, help them understand the importance of mental and physical health in their career management.

CHAPTER 9

Professional Development

Develop a passion for learning. If you do, you will never cease to grow.
—Anthony J. D'Angelo

I'm a constant learner. You need to be a constant student because things change and you have to change and grow. And I emphasize the word "grow."
—Zig Ziglar

In order to serve our clients best, it is important we stay current in our field. Those of us holding professional credentials like the GCDF, CCSP, or CCC are required to complete continuing education hours. But regardless of whether or not you hold a credential, it is important to continue to learn. Staying up to date in career development is a key piece to raising your credibility—and the credibility of the entire career profession.

Over the years I have observed colleagues in many different fields and realized there are those people who attend and present at conferences, network with others, read journals, and work at their own growth and knowledge base to improve services to their clients ... and then there are others who work as if they have already reached their professional pinnacle.

It has always been important to me to be the former. Maybe it's because I am a huge extrovert and my need to process information out loud leads me to connect with others any way I can. Maybe I still suffer from the 'imposter syndrome' and feel I must be involved so I can learn more. I do know it has always been important for me to learn more so I can do my job better. Despite it not always being easy, this has meant reading professional journals (hard to find the time), attending conferences (hard to find the money), taking classes (hard to find the time and money), and networking with other like-minded professionals (sometimes hard in a rural state like Maine).

What I've found over the years is most of the people who really *want* to do some of these activities are busy people—very busy people. So how do they find the time?

Learning Through Reading

One way is to get (and stay) organized and then carve out time each week to commit to learning something new. When I was working a more typical 40-hour work week, I had a standing "appointment" in my calendar on Mondays at 4:00 p.m. to read the *Chronicle of Higher Education* or a journal of my choice. Did I do it every week? No. But I can tell you I did it frequently, and I always felt better when I took that 15 minutes out of a busy day to read something that often gave me a broader perspective I needed. It was uncanny how I gravitated to articles that seemed to address a current issue I was having in my work life. Perspective is so important.

According to a speed-reading test sponsored by Staples as part of an e-book promotion, the average adult reads at 300 words per minute. (Source Forbes – read article here http://bit.ly/peakcareers117). In 15 minutes, the average person can read 4,500 words. You can gain a lot of content in that time. Take your speed-reading test here http://bit.ly/peakcareers116

Another great time saver in my busy world that helps keep me on top of current news is the app and website Feedly, which helps me organize blogs, newspapers, and online articles by categories so I can do a quick view of my sorted list and select the articles I want to read or peruse quickly.

I also try to have at least one or two "professional" books waiting for me either on my shelf or my Kindle reader, with pleasure reading books that I mix in. While reading books, I like to jot down notes and possible things "to do" generated from the reading. Then I write short reviews on my book blog, which helps me when I want to recommend a book to a client, colleague, or friend. It also helps me remember which books I've read :-) To see what books I've read, go to https://peak-careers.com/category/book-reviews/.

I encourage you to read professional books, magazines, journals, or blogs as a way of expanding your own professional development. Reading is just one way you can learn something new or discover a different way of doing things you've been doing for long time. As a reader, I ultimately hope I will learn something to help my clients.

Another advantage of reading is to slow you down and take you away from our often-overstimulating technological world. So much of the information on the web Is written in short messages, which are more like "sound bites." A longer journal article or book will really help expand and stimulate your thinking.

I challenge you, as I do myself, to carve out time and break away from the technology at work to read for 15 minutes, 30 minutes, or an hour each day. Let's make a commitment to improve ourselves and continue to learn so we can better serve our clients. Challenge yourself to grow, to think differently by reading different views, to try and understand others (especially if you don't agree with them), and to learn something new.

> My book goal: Read 15-30 minutes each day
>
> What could your book goal be?
>
> _____

Books are not the only place we should be reading. **There are many great career-oriented journals or magazines** published by a wide variety professional associations, both online and in print. Here are a few of my favorites.

National Career Development Association

- Career Convergence, an online magazine. Articles are mostly under 950 words (3 minutes of reading for the average person). Fairly quick reads, broken into constituent groups. You can search by various constituent groups as well.
- Here is my recent Independent Practice article on Using Social Media in Private Practice. http://bit.ly/peakcareers118. Check out

your constituent group while you are there.

- *Career Developments*, a hard copy quarterly journal for members only. Most articles are around 1,200 words (4 minutes of reading for the average person).

National Academic Advising Association

- *Academic Advising Today*, a quarterly online magazine. Articles are an average length of 1,000-1,500 words (less than 5 minutes of reading for most of us).
- Check out one of my favorite articles I wrote a few years ago comparing academic advisors (and career advisors) to the Wizard of Oz http://bit.ly/12nmpIA

Life Planning Network

- Quarterly e-journal focusing on working with Boomers. Articles are an average length of about 1,000 words (about 3-4 minutes of reading).

As you can see, these are really not a huge commitment of time ... you just need to take the time.

I also encourage you to read outside of our profession. I like to browse a variety of different magazines in bookstores, like *Inc.* or *Backpacker* or *Time*, and flip through to see any articles of interest. This is my "intentional serendipity" approach to discovering something by accident. It is good to see what people *outside* our profession are writing about careers.

My professional journal reading goal:
Save them up and read for about an hour each Friday

What could your journal goal be?

_____

Learning Through Seminars

As career practitioners it is our responsibility to continue to learn and grow in order to serve our clients best. I was talking with a client and he said, "I can't believe how much the process of finding jobs has changed!" Clearly, he was frustrated he could not just open the newspaper, find a job opening, and apply with a resume. It is my job to know the current practices in my profession. It is my job to stay "fresh." It is my job to be inspired to do good work, so I can provide the *best services* to my clients.

For people who have good size budgets for professional development, that may mean attending the National Career Development Association conferences or taking classes or seminars. Those with little financial support for professional development need to be more creative.

TED Talks are a great, *free* way to continue to learn and grow.
- Often, they are people you would see at national conferences
- They are "bite-sized" too, between 10-20 minutes
- They are inspirational and often challenge us to do better
- The diverse range of speaker presentation styles is always helpful to identify strategies for improving your own presentation skills

Take 15 minutes each week and put in your earbuds and find a TED Talk that inspires you to be your best or gives you a different angle on a familiar topic. We can all find 15 minutes. Yeah, I know you are busy, but seriously, you can find 15–20 minutes *somewhere* in your 40+ hour workweek.

What about using a TED Talk for staff development? Why not take 20–30 minutes out of your staff meetings once a month to have the entire staff to watch and then discuss a TED Talk? This is where you can grow your team, get to know people better, and possibly provide better service to your students/clients as a result. Have each staff member take a turn at choosing a TED Talk.

No matter what you do, take the 15-20 minutes and keep yourself energized, learning, and growing.

I sent out a survey in 2019 asking colleagues and friends for their favorite TED Talks and how they used them with their clients. You can find the results on my site here http://bit.ly/peakcareers104

Special thanks to all of you who took the time to fill this out. I now have a few more **"20 minute bite sized professional developments"** to watch.

I created my five-week, discussion-based, online seminars because I felt strongly we need to continue to grow and learn in our profession. But I wanted something different than a passive, independent study-type online class. I wanted engagement. I also wanted something that was affordable and flexible so people could log in when they wanted to, without set times to meet. Rarely do I have the same time each week available. Check them out at https://peak-careers.com

Learning Through Podcasts

A few years ago, a person in my Boomer online seminar turned me onto a podcast called *Meditation Oasis* that has a number of different meditations. My favorite is called "Relax into Sleep." Then last summer I was talking with Marc Miller of Career Pivot via video-conference. He talked about how he was listening to a number of different podcasts when he walked to the coffee shop, and how much he felt he was learning daily because of it.

I have added more than 20 different podcasts to my regular listening. I might listen to 2–4 different ones each week. I could not possibly listen to all 20, but they are there if I want them. They range from a few that focus on entrepreneurship and marketing topics, to a number that focus on career topics. Of course, there are many others that cover news and entertainment. Sometimes I'll listen while I'm working out or while walking in the neighborhood on one of my daily breaks, or I will just take a half hour and sit and listen to a podcast because I may want to take notes.

Here are a few of my favorites.

Marketing:
- *Agents of Change*
- *Build Your Own Brand* with Ryan Rhoten
- *PR Maven* with Nancy Marshall
- *ProBlogger*

Entrepreneurship
- *Entrepreneurs on Fire* with John Lee Dumas
- *The Tim Ferris Show*

Career
- *First, You Hustle* (Columbus College of Art & Design, but great career advice for all college students)

- *Repurpose Your Career* with Marc Miller (focus is on Boomers)
- *The Voice of the Job Seekers* with Mark Anthony Dyson

Fun stuff
- *Meditation Oasis*
- *The Science of Happiness*
- *Spittin' Chiclets* (hockey talk)
- *Hidden Brain*
- *Serial*

Regardless of when and how you do it, **I strongly encourage you to add podcasts to your professional development modes of learning.**

Learning Through Professional Associations

Regardless of where I have worked, I have been involved with my professional associations.

While in graduate school and into my career as a Director of Student Activities, I was active in the Association of College Unions-International (ACU-I). I presented at regional conferences and even wrote an article published in ACU-I comparing student governments in New Zealand and Australia to the American model. (This was a great way to rationalize a gap year backpacking/hitchhiking around New Zealand and Australia after grad school).

In my short stint in the Office of Tourism for the State of Maine, I presented to a number of groups in the tourism industry. As a high school guidance counselor, I was involved with the Maine Vocational Association (MVA), Maine Counseling Association (MeCA), and Maine School Counselor Association (MESCA) at Board levels and even as president of MESCA. I am a two-time past president of Maine Career Development Association (MCDA). I am serving, or have served, on two committees for the National Career Development Association. I have learned so much from all of these.

But this is not simply about "being involved" for my own extroverted self. Here is why you might want to consider being more involved with your professional association(s).

You'll practice lifelong learning
I know, you've heard this before, but in the world we live in today, things change so much and so fast it is important to stay ahead of the learning

curve. By attending conferences, you continue to learn. If I pick up even one new idea in a session or a keynote it is worthwhile. But some sessions are even life-changing, like when I heard John Krumboltz present on the Happenstance Learning Theory, which lead to my thinking of 'intentional serendipity.'

Other sessions might have a small tidbit about how to better organize an event. Regardless, questioning what I am doing, hearing how others do similar things, and learning about new technology to improve my "reach" to others are all *great* reasons to attend a conference—you might just discover something by accident to make you a better career counselor or coach.

You'll gain leadership skills

There are many opportunities for us locally, statewide, regionally, and/or nationally to be involved with our professions. Not everyone aspires to be the president of an association, but I encourage you to be more than "just a member." Membership is the first step to expose you to your profession, but then take it one step further to volunteering for activities. Every conference needs people to help at registration, collect evaluations, and make sure presenters are all set in their rooms—all easy ways to be involved. And for you introverts, there is no better way to meet others in your profession than to volunteer to serve on a committee or help out. It gives you a focus and a way to meet new people.

For many, getting to the volunteering level will be it. Others who never thought they'd go further often find a leadership role that fits them well, giving them the confidence to move on and spread their wings a bit more. Most people who end up in leadership roles say they never expected themselves to be there but are *never* disappointed they did. Just as we tell our clients, getting involved with others is a great way to learn your strengths and weaknesses.

You'll get the chance to network (*relationship build*)

I see networking as a symbiotic relationship. You need to give as much as you get.

You are likely to have a number of different jobs, often in different industries, over your career. Because "job security" is a thing of the past, developing and owning your own "career security" is critical to your future. Networking with others is the best way to prepare for your next move. Your next job will likely be the result of someone in your network telling you about a position, and then encouraging you to apply to one or even creating a position for you. At a minimum, the power of gaining knowledge from a network of people can be exponential compared to what you can learn by yourself.

You also need to view yourself as a person who also helps others. Giving out advice, information, or potential leads to people in your network is important. If you look to help people, you will view "networking" as a dual relationship, not just as a way to receive your own benefits.

Networking can also involve the opportunity to mentor new people in the field. I see this as different from the point above—as intentionally looking at people who are new to our field, often younger, who might need a nudge to improve their skills, gain more confidence, and avoid some of the common pitfalls of being new in our profession. Most of us had people we looked up to and emulated in some ways who taught us important lessons. Even if you are new to the field yourself, you can be helpful to others who are coming in next year.

When I was the President of Maine Career Development Association (MCDA), I felt strongly about engaging members, developing future leaders of our associations, collaborating with other organizations, and improving member benefits in order to create a vibrant association and a place for career professionals to grow. By having each Board member take on a committee they were interested in, our Board members were engaged in the association. I also divided up our membership and assigned about 10 members to each Board member. Their job was to reach out and engage the members and to personalize the relationship a little bit more.

Our committees and work groups also had MCDA members volunteering on them. This last point is how you prepare for future leaders and find ways for members to be involved. This can be as simple as working at a registration table for the conference and is their introduction to the association, which often grows over time.

Career Coach Tips

- Commit to your own professional development and be a lifelong learner so you can be the best career service provider possible.
- Find time weekly to devote 15 minutes to either reading books or journals, listening to podcasts, or watching videos to enhance your knowledge.
- Engage in your profession by attending local, regional, or national conferences and find ways to volunteer in order to get the most out of this experience as possible.
- Consider taking classes, seminars, webinars, or other learning experiences to further your understanding of career topics.

CHAPTER 10

Private Practice

In thinking of taking a risk and branching out to explore a woodworking passion, my 9 year old nephew said "Don't be scared. Just try it, Auntie. You might like it.

—Jackie Giannakoulis

"When you choose to take the road less traveled, it can sometimes be a bumpy ride along the way, but if you're doing it for the right reasons, then the reward is so great."

—Gretchen Bleiler

Do or do not; there is no try

—Yoda

"Twenty years from now you will be more disappointed by the things you didn't do than by the ones you did. So throw off the bowlines, sail away from the safe harbor, catch the trade winds in your sails. Explore. Dream. Discover."

—Mark Twain

I know that many career counselors, academic advisors, and other career service providers often consider going into private practice, so I want to use this chapter to give some thoughts and tips. I began Peak-Careers Consulting part-time around 2000 while working full time at Kennebec Valley Community College. There is no way I could have gone into a full-time private practice at that point in time. I needed to test the waters and see what worked. And while it's true what worked in 2000 is quite different than what is working in 2015, there are many lessons I learned I hope will be helpful to anyone considering starting their own private practice.

First thing to know: **it's not for the weak of heart**. It is a lot of work. And much of the work has little to do with career services. You have to be the marketer, bookkeeper, custodian … and occasionally you get to do career services. One of the most difficult things for me to get used to after a 25+ year career of being paid bi-weekly with full benefits was never knowing when I would get paid. But it's all been worth it, and I could never work for someone again after having the freedom to do my own thing.

First: decide your purpose

What makes you unique in the marketplace. Sound familiar? The same process we ask our clients/students to go through to identify skills, passions, and interests is the one you need to practice yourself.

You must be something that is "true" to yourself. You can't be everything to everyone. Figure out what makes you unique. What is your value-added statement? Who is your audience? Be as specific as you can. For me, I choose the tagline **"Promoting the development of career professionals"** because I wanted to reach as many individuals as possible to help them find work that satisfied them, and I am inspired to train people to better serve their clients. I love the educational side of career development and I want it to be "engaging." From that my Facilitating Career Development (FCD) class become my initial offering, and then I added online seminars for career practitioners. My slogan has evolved to **"Professional Development for Career Practitioners"** but my *purpose* has not changed.

Over the years many people have told me to make my online seminars 'independent study' style, where people can login and complete them whenever they want. I've actually thought about it—it would be **much** easier on my end. Then I think about the loss of the **engagement** that is so important to me in the discussions between career practitioners in the seminars. When I go back to my purpose and passion, I realize the discussion-based seminars are who I am. By having a clear vision of purpose and passion I can keep my business consistent and clear to my mission.

I'm not saying you should not ever modify and adjust your practice. When I revisited my first business plan after about 18 months (more on this later), I was shocked at what I had *thought* I was going to be doing compared with what I *actually* was doing. For example, I thought I would be working primarily with the Boomer population and had 500 brochures printed up to reach this audience. Turns out most of my clients are mid-life career changers and recent college graduates. (I have about 400 brochures left if anyone wants them).

Create a business plan

Every state has a Small Business Development Center (SDC) funded by the federal Department of Labor. I highly recommend you meet with someone in your area. They have a wealth of resources and knowledge… and it is all free. The first thing my SBDC contact had me do was a business plan. The process of writing things down clarifies your thinking. The Certified Business Counselor I worked with had me identify competitors, describe my value in the marketplace, define what problem I solve, and more. Then she had me put together a budget projection—how much money I will make each month and from what income stream. I thought I'd done a great job, but when I reviewed it with her, she pointed out that I was "out of money in July." Yikes! Because I teach the FCD class in October I tend to collect most of the payments in August. I had not considered that fully when putting my budget together.

Having an outside expert (all free by the way), I was able to refine my plan. When I asked her how the heck I was supposed to predict what would sell each month, she told me I should make my best guess and then I had to believe it. What!? How does that work? Well, I can tell you that it does. In the fall of 2015, I looked at my 2015 projections and was astounded that in two areas I was within 10% of my goals financially! "Where focus goes, energy flows."

Once you have a plan, you need to pull it out and look at it annually, making adjustments where needed. Stay focused on what is working. Get rid of the things that are not. This is similar to my mantra I use with clients on setting their goals. Revisit your goals every three months and **"revise, recommit, or remove."** Often things will need to be revised—so do it. Some things you will recommit to because they are working and remain in your purpose and vision. And … some things should be removed. Just "let it go."

Small Business Development Centers (SBDCs) provide assistance to small businesses and aspiring entrepreneurs throughout the United States and its territories. SBDCs help entrepreneurs realize the dream of business ownership and help existing businesses remain competitive in a complex, ever-changing global marketplace. SBDCs are hosted by leading universities and state economic development agencies, and funded in part through a partnership with SBA.

SBDC advisors provide aspiring and current small business owners a variety of free business consulting and low-cost training services including business plan development, manufacturing assistance, financial packaging and lending assistance, exporting and importing support, disaster recovery assistance, procurement and contracting aid, market research help, 8(a) program support, and healthcare guidance.

Find your closest center here:
https://www.sba.gov/tools/local-assistance/sbdc.

Establish an online presence

This seems obvious to me but I'll say it anyway. Get your own website. You should not rely upon any platform that you do not own. Get a domain name that is your name when possible. Peak-Careers.com is what I choose because I wanted the word "careers" in my domain. The "Peak" was actually my nickname growing up. My friends called me "Peak" and "Peaker," and I like the image of climbing a mountain in your own career development. In general, I recommend you have a business and website that has your name in it when possible.

Set SMART goals

Just like we do with our clients, set your goals for what is realistic. Make sure they are measurable. You can use the **SMART** acronym: Specific, Measurable, Action-Oriented, Realistic, and Time-specific. Once you know **what you want to accomplish** then you need to determine **how you will measure it**.

Below you can see my first few years of data I collected from Google Analytics. I determined the information I wanted to know was how many "Users" were coming to my website and aimed to increase that number each year.

	January 2014	January 2015	January 2016
Sessions	412	709	891
Users	335	559	739
Pageviews	945	1634	1751
Pages/Session	2.29	2.3	1.97
Avg. Session Duration	1.47	2.12	1.43
Bounce rate*	60.70%	57.40%	67.34%
New Sessions	74%	71%	73%
New visitors	73.80%	70.90%	73.50%

*Bounce rate is the percentage of single page visits (or web sessions). It is the percentage of visits in which a person leaves your website from the landing page without browsing any further. Google Analytics calculates and report the bounce rate on a website.

Once you have the data, then you need to analyze it. Why did the bounce rate go down in January 2015? Did I have a more interesting blog that specific month? Did I include more links to other pages on my website in that article which kept them on my site? The answers to these questions then guide me on what to do in the future.

I also track how many people *open* my Constant Contact monthly newsletter and how many people *click* on whatever links I have to my website. From this I can determine my best subject lines and blogs that seem to interest my audience and then produce more content my followers want to read. Without data, I'd never know.

As a Myers-Briggs ENFP typology, I am not very interested in data. I am more interested in "feelings" and "helping people." But it just makes sense to pay attention to what is working and owning my own business has forced me to pay attention to the details. There is so much more data I could analyze in Google Analytics, Facebook Insights, Twitter Analytics, but you have to decide what you need as a minimum. It can be overwhelming because there is so much information at your fingertips in all these platforms. I recommend finding specific data points and measuring them for a while to see if there are trends or specific things you can do to influence them. Then you can build up to more information if needed.

I have quite a bit of data on my website activity, my Peak-Careers Facebook page, and my Constant Contact emails since 2014. And when it comes time to look ahead and plan, set goals, and try to figure out what is working, I have actual data to look at to help me.

Seek advice

I know I am not an expert on everything, specifically topics like SEO, bounce rates, the research behind all the various career theories, marketing, and many other topics. Sure, I have learned a lot over the years. But I also am very comfortable asking for help and advice. When you start your business, seek the advice of the Small Business Administration people in your area—but don't stop there.

I created an Advisory Board of six people who I meet with about three times each year to give me feedback and ideas on moving forward. I identified people who have different perspectives and serve different clientele, and can bring some diversity to me. For example, I realized a few years ago that I did not have any Millennials on my Board, so I looked for some younger people to join me. I also noticed that I was relying heavily on people who worked in higher education. And although this population makes up a large segment of my clients, I asked myself "What else am I missing?"

These Advisory Board members are all over the country, but with the power of the Zoom video-conference platform we meet three times each year (one of the three meetings is done one-on-one with each person). I also have them give me feedback on blogs as I write them. However you choose to get feedback and advice is fine. Your clientele may be much more local, so you could reach out to local business leaders and meet locally. You may want to look at your Chamber of Commerce and local service organizations like Rotary Club to find out who the leaders are in your area and develop a relationship with these folks.

In the spring of 2017, I hired a business coach. Not cheap. I was reluctant to hire a coach and spend all that money, but it has proven to be another good investment. My coach is an outside person to my field who can give me suggestions on how to improve the business side of Peak-Careers. She has helped me grow my email list, create marketing materials, and most importantly change my "language" of selling what I offer by improving my email subject lines and marketing messages.

I have also met with my local SCORE mentor. SCORE (www.score.org) offers free business advice from seasoned businesspeople. My mentor there asked me questions to get me thinking about the important issues that arise when running a business. Even though he did not know my industry or have experience in online education, he was able to help me look at my profit-and-loss reports and help me understand my bandwidth to provide my services.

Having worked in higher education and public education most of my career, I found that I needed to hear different perspectives from business-people like the Small Business Administration, SCORE, and a business coach in order to run the strongest business possible.

Know, like, and trust takes time

Being a solopreneur can be lonely. I work in isolation for much of my day. When I first started full time with Peak-Careers in February of 2012, I was astounded at how many hours I spent each week doing tasks that I did *not* get paid for! I was crafting and sending emails, writing a monthly newsletter, writing blogs, working on my budget, going to professional association meetings, and more. You don't get paid for any of that. *"Holy smokes, how am I ever going to make this work?"*

I was talking to a few other private practice people who had been in the business for a while, and they both said that you need to spend about 70% of your time talking with people, thinking, writing, etc., in order to spend 30% delivering paid content. Wow—that was shocking but clearly true for me.

The majority of my time is spent on tasks and duties whose sole purpose is to help others "know, like, and trust me." People want to buy from, hire, and spend time with people they **know, like, and trust.** It is not as much about the pricing and the content as this "feeling" factor. So, you need to spend time being consistent with your message and find ways to get that authentic "you" message out there. I not only spend my time on LinkedIn, Twitter, and Facebook, but I am also involved with my Chamber of Commerce and the National Career Development Association, volunteering in a number of different capacities. I am also willing to meet whenever I can with my peers in the career field who have questions. You have to give a lot in order to receive.

I also need to spend time doing work that I simply do **not want to do**, i.e., the dirty work. Accept and embrace the fact you will not be doing what you love to do all the time. If I could do workshops, classes, and trainings 30 hours a week, I would be ecstatic. But when you own your own business, you are the bookkeeper, marketer, receptionist, and custodian, as well as the professional who delivers quality services. **Find time each week to do the things you don't like to do. Accept it. Get it done, so you can do what you want to do.** Lots of businesspeople fail because they have not done a good job on some of these details.

Don't be afraid to spend money

You need to spend money to make money. Coming from education I was always trying to save a buck and find the most inexpensive way of doing things. This is a good trait, but sometimes you need to spend money in order to demonstrate "quality." I wanted to do a big change in my website years ago and had three bids: one for $700, one for $1,000, and one for nearly $2,000. I went with the $2,000 because they asked me 100 more questions than either of the first two. They worked *very* hard to understand me and put their proposal together. Turns out, years later I still have people complimenting me on my website, i.e., my storefront.

If you find yourself putting things off on your "to do" list all the time, it might be time to consider contracting that task out to someone else. In the spring of 2015 I found myself doing so many mundane tasks that I could not afford to pay anyone else to do. Well ... I could not afford to *not* pay someone else to do it. I hired a virtual assistant, which allowed me to focus on the tasks that I love to do ... and get paid to do. My V.A. would work 1 or 2 hours per week, and I was free to move on to bigger and better things. She now works closer to 4 hours per week and I have a second V.A. who works about 3 hours per week, freeing me up to do the things I love to do.

How did I find my V.A.? Just like most small businesses do. I asked my network if they knew anyone who might be looking for a side gig registering people for events, updating my website, and helping me out with my online learning management platform. Lo and behold, I found someone who lives up the road from me.

Find balance

I've always worked hard for every employer I ever had, and when I started Peak-Careers it was the same ... lots of hours for my employer :) Yet you have to balance your life too. *All work and no play makes Jack a dull boy.* I love that my work day begins and ends when I say it does. If I want to take a walk after breakfast, I can. If I want to run errands in the middle of the day (which is great because there's not as many people), I can. Sometimes this means I need to work in the evening to get things done, but it is *my* time to decide how to spend. For a while I was working closer to 60 hours /week, which I needed to early on when I was full time with Peak-Careers. But you have to find a way to balance your life out while still making money. I try not to work on weekends and evenings. If I do, I keep it very short. I do something physical every day: going for a walk, playing hockey, lifting weights, or Qi Gong—something to break up my computer time.

Market yourself

So you know who you are and who you serve. Now how do you get the word out? You can pay for ads, but you want to know that your audience is receiving the information and you are getting the return on investment you hope for. I have bought Facebook ads and really did not see much benefit. I plan to explore Google Ads as well. I also will buy ad space in the Maine Career Development Association conference bulletin or the Maine Counseling Association newsletter because I know this is the audience I am trying to reach and they are the organizations I want to support. But I don't buy many other ads.

With social media at your fingertips and your goal of driving people to your website to "purchase" services, you really must have an online presence. (Sound familiar? I am often telling my coaching clients that same thing).

The question you must answer first is, **Where are my clients hanging out?** My audience is career practitioners, and they are mostly on LinkedIn connecting and learning from others. A bunch are on Twitter, and many also have a Facebook account. They are also on Reddit, Snapchat, YouTube, Pinterest, Instagram, Tumblr, Flickr, Quora, Periscope, and more.

Find which networks your clients are on, pick the top three, and focus your energy there. Don't try to be on all of them at once—it can't be done. For the three you choose, make sure you maximize your time and effort. For example, I am on LinkedIn daily sharing, posting, commenting, liking, and reading. I have a weekly plan for LinkedIn that ensures I post something at least once a day in addition to my regular "like, share, and comment" on other people's posts.

For example, once a month I write a blog I post on my website. I then push that out on LinkedIn three times the first week, two times the second week, and once the third week. I do this so I reach different people who are on LinkedIn at different times. I also share content from other bloggers at a minimum of twice a week, *plus* any content I stumble on that looks interesting. I have a similar plan for Twitter and Facebook. I use the Hootsuite platform to schedule most of my posting each week so it is spread out over the week and posted at different times throughout the day.

Think about it. If I post something on Twitter at 8 a.m. Monday morning and you don't go to Twitter until 10 a.m., it's likely you will miss my post. If I post something on LinkedIn at 8 a.m. Monday and you don't go to LinkedIn until the afternoon, you are likely to miss it. By pushing content out throughout the day and week, I am more likely to reach my audience. Consistency is important, which is why having a plan is critical.

I create a weekly marketing calendar. You can put this in a Google calendar, in an Excel sheet listing the weeks, and/or on a wall calendar in your office. However you do it, you will want to plan out as far as possible. I personally try to stay three months out, but I know another consultant who plans out his entire year. As an ENFP Myers-Briggs person, that is mind blowing to think about!

I send out emails every Tuesday. My current marketing calendar for December shows:

1st Tuesday—Write / post blog on reading books for professional development

2nd Tuesday—Newsletter with book recommendations

3rd Tuesday—Interview at least two people on why they read books for their professional development

4th Tuesday—Repurpose old blog on LinkedIn

When I look at my calendar, I can see visually what I need to be working on for the upcoming weeks. I plan this out for three months and revisit it on my monthly "retreat" day. I'll modify things and move things around based upon need, but I have a plan. I can also anticipate holidays or special events coming up, which helps me think about tailored marketing ideas.

How and where to share your expertise

My goal is to provide content that interests my clients. Sometimes it is my own content in a blog, article, or newsletter, but often it is sharing other people's content. Or it might be simply chiming in with thoughts to a discussion that "add value" to the topic. You want to be "present" where your clients are hanging out and provide them content they are looking for, while showing people you know what you are talking about. This is how they "know, like, and trust" you.

The content I share is very similar across all my social media sites, but I might reword my posts/comments to fit each site. Here are my thoughts on the main sites I use.

1. LinkedIn: This is a great professional community made up of people who want to help each other—much like at professional conferences like National Career Development Association, when you meet others and offer help or seek help. LinkedIn has been around for a while; I have been on it since December 2007, becoming more active as I felt comfortable. Besides the ability to present yourself in a professional light on your profile, the site features numerous groups you can join and participate in to advance your learning. And more importantly, you can use LinkedIn as a springboard to create your online presence.

2. Facebook: Facebook can be a little more playful than LinkedIn. There, I have a personal page and a Peak-Careers business page where I can share a post or article (Look for PeakCareers on Facebook!). I try to share content on my business page that career practitioners would like to see and tend to post more in the late afternoon or evening here. Facebook also now allows me to schedule and boost posts on my business page. I have also played around with Facebook Live, choosing career topics of interest to me, and have gained some positive results from the Live sessions. It's still too early to tell the impact of my Facebook Live sessions, but I encourage you to try things to see if they work for you.

3. Twitter: It's hard to believe you can share content in 280 characters *and* network with others on this platform. Someone once told me it is not about *how many* people you follow, but more about finding the people aggregating the information you are looking for and then following them. Because you can follow anyone, and they can follow you, Twitter is also much more playful than LinkedIn, but it's still a great place to share content, learn, and network. This is a great area for me, as I am always looking for career practitioners who are comfortable online to consider taking my online seminars. I also have a few favorite Twitter Chats that I will join occasionally. #InternPro #LinkedInChat #CareerServChat and a few others.

4. Pinterest: My virtual assistant is personally on Pinterest, and she suggested a business presence there for Peak-Careers. This is still a work in progress, but I have already seen some traction. I also use Pins to support my blogs and newsletters so there is a visual aspect to what I am writing about.

The key to using social media strategically is to find out where *your* clients are hanging out—then establish a presence there.

I strongly suggest having a **marketing strategy** for each of your social media sites and to be in it for the long run. I started LinkedIn in 2007 and decided to go slowly and only add people I knew or who added value to my business. I also know other private practitioners who will add anyone and everyone and are surprised with my approach. Both are right.

I added Facebook next, then Twitter, then Pinterest, and G+ (now defunct). Each time I went slowly and made time on a regular basis to explore, watch, participate, and add people to that network. No one says you have to do it like anyone else, but you do want to spend some time to figure out the culture and expectations of each platform. The amount of time I spend on each platform is different. I spend most of my time on LinkedIn because that is where my customers are hanging out. Many are on Twitter, but I don't spend as much time there because I don't feel like I get as much "engagement," and engagement is what I am after. Engagement lasts and has "reach" online. My advice is to devise a strategy and be willing to change as needed.

How much time to devote to your social media presence is entirely up to you. I try to spend 15–20 minutes in the morning and about the same later in the day—sometimes more, sometimes less, but my goal is to have a presence online daily. I have a few tools that help me accomplish this.

1. Feedly: Feedly.com allows me to track other bloggers and websites and to categorize them in a daily feed. I can log into Feedly in the morning and peruse all the career bloggers I am following. Then I skim the news feeds I follow and quickly see if there is any content I want to share with my followers on any (or all) of my social media sites.

2. Hootsuite.com: The free version of Hootsuite allows me to schedule posts on three social media sites. I can literally find content on Feedly (or my own) and schedule out the week on Twitter, Facebook, and LinkedIn in about 20 minutes.

Career Coach Tips

- Find out where your customers/clients are hanging out and provide them content they are looking for to establish yourself as an expert in your field.
- Remember the key is to have a presence online that drives people to your website where they can "buy" your services.
- Have a presence where your customers are hanging out, be consistent, and give them a reason to "know, like, and trust" you.

Epilogue

I hope this book gave you some points to think about, tips on improving your work, ideas on getting out of your comfort zone, and advice on professional development. As you improve, you advance our entire profession. As I said in the preface, my goal is to reach the greatest numbers of people and help them in their career development. When you improve your skills, everyone you come into contact benefits from your knowledge and experience.

Thank you for being committed to your own professional development.

Please connect with me on LinkedIn, Twitter, and other social media platforms where you find me. I would love to hear from you and your thoughts on this book. Your feedback only makes me better.

https://www.linkedin.com/in/peakcareers/

https://twitter.com/PeakCareers

https://www.facebook.com/PeakCareers/

JimPeacock@Peak-Careers.com

https://peak-careers.com